New Directions for Adult and Continuing Education

Susan Imel
Jovita M. Ross-Gordon
COEDITORS-IN-CHIEF

Swimming Upstream: Black Males in Adult Education

Dionne Rosser-Mims
Joni Schwartz
Brendaly Drayton
Talmadge C. Guy
EDITORS

Number 144 • Winter 2014
Jossey-Bass
San Francisco

SWIMMING UPSTREAM: BLACK MALES IN ADULT EDUCATION
Dionne Rosser-Mims, Joni Schwartz, Brendaly Drayton, Talmadge C. Guy (eds)
New Directions for Adult and Continuing Education, no. 144
Susan Imel, Jovita M. Ross-Gordon, Coeditors-in-Chief

© 2014 Wiley Periodicals, Inc., A Wiley Company. All rights reserved. No part of this publication may be reproduced, stored in a retrieval system, or transmitted in any form or by any means, electronic, mechanical, photocopying, recording, scanning, or otherwise, except as permitted under Section 107 or 108 of the 1976 United States Copyright Act, without either the prior written permission of the Publisher or authorization through payment of the appropriate per-copy fee to the Copyright Clearance Center, 222 Rosewood Drive, Danvers, MA 01923, (978) 750-8400, fax (978) 646-8600. The copyright notice appearing at the bottom of the first page of an article in this journal indicates the copyright holder's consent that copies may be made for personal or internal use, or for personal or internal use of specific clients, on the condition that the copier pay for copying beyond that permitted by law. This consent does not extend to other kinds of copying, such as copying for distribution, for advertising or promotional purposes, for creating collective works, or for resale. Such permission requests and other permission inquiries should be addressed to the Permissions Department, c/o John Wiley & Sons, Inc., 111 River Street, Hoboken, NJ 07030; (201) 748-6011, fax (201) 748-6008, www.wiley.com/go/permissions.

Microfilm copies of issues and articles are available in 16mm and 35mm, as well as microfiche in 105mm, through University Microfilms Inc., 300 North Zeeb Road, Ann Arbor, Michigan 48106-1346.

NEW DIRECTIONS FOR ADULT AND CONTINUING EDUCATION (ISSN 1052-2891, electronic ISSN 1536-0717) is part of The Jossey-Bass Higher and Adult Education Series and is published quarterly by Wiley Subscription Services, Inc., A Wiley Company, at Jossey-Bass, One Montgomery Street, Suite 1200, San Francisco, CA 94104-4594. POSTMASTER: Send address changes to New Directions for Adult and Continuing Education, Jossey-Bass, One Montgomery Street, Suite 1200, San Francisco, CA 94104-4594.

New Directions for Adult and Continuing Education is indexed in CIJE: Current Index to Journals in Education (ERIC); Contents Pages in Education (T&F); ERIC Database (Education Resources Information Center); Higher Education Abstracts (Claremont Graduate University); and Sociological Abstracts (CSA/CIG).

INDIVIDUAL SUBSCRIPTION RATE (in USD): $89 per year US/Can/Mex, $113 rest of world; institutional subscription rate: $335 US, $375 Can/Mex, $409 rest of world. Single copy rate: $29. Electronic only–all regions: $89 individual, $335 institutional; Print & Electronic–US: $98 individual, $402 institutional; Print & Electronic–Canada/Mexico: $98 individual, $442 institutional; Print & Electronic–Rest of World: $122 individual, $476 institutional.

EDITORIAL CORRESPONDENCE should be sent to the Coeditors-in-Chief, Susan Imel, 3076 Woodbine Place, Columbus, Ohio 43202-1341, e-mail: imel.l@osu.edu; or Jovita M. Ross-Gordon, Southwest Texas State University, CLAS Dept., 601 University Drive, San Marcos, TX 78666.

Cover design: Wiley
Cover Images: © Lava 4 images | Shutterstock

www.josseybass.com

Contents

EDITORS' NOTES 1
Dionne Rosser-Mims, Joni Schwartz, Brendaly Drayton, Talmadge C. Guy

1. Race, the Black Male, and Heterogeneous Racisms in Education 5
Juanita Johnson-Bailey, Nichole Ray, Tennille Lasker-Scott
This chapter explores the effects of historical and current racism on the educational experiences of American Black males. The authors use critical race theory to illustrate how assumptions about culture and gender have subverted the egalitarian ideals of adult education. Teachers and students are urged to use critical reflection and open discussion about racial issues.

2. The (End)angered Black Male Swimming Against the Current 15
Talmadge C. Guy
This chapter discusses the sociohistorical and deeply embedded myths and stereotypes that have dominated narratives about Black men and how these shape the educational and professional experiences of Black men.

3. The Good Provider: Missing or Overlooked? 27
Brendaly Drayton
This chapter explores Black men's reasons for participating in an adult basic education and literacy program through the lens of gender identity.

4. High School Equivalency as Counter-Space 37
Joni Schwartz
This chapter is based on the findings of an ethnographic study of an urban General Education Development (GED®) program and suggests that, for some marginalized African American and other young men of color, adult education programs are counter-spaces (Yosso, Ceja, Smith, & Solorzano, 2009) of spatial justice in opposition to previous negative school spaces. The chapter is framed from the perspective of critical race theory.

5. A New Normal: Young Men of Color, Trauma, and Engagement in Learning 49
Carlyle Van Thompson, Paul J. Schwartz
This chapter will center on the continuing impact of systemic and persistent educational trauma experienced by Black and Latino males and how trauma affects their current learning. The young men's counterstories from a phenomenological study and documentary are included.

6. The Reentry Adult College Student: An Exploration of the 59
Black Male Experience
Dionne Rosser-Mims, Glenn A. Palmer, Pamela Harroff
This chapter shares findings from a qualitative study on reentry adult Black males' postsecondary education experiences and identifies strategies to help this population matriculate through college and graduate.

7. Returning to School After Incarceration: Policy, Prisoners, and 69
the Classroom
Brian Miller, Joserichsen Mondesir, Timothy Stater, Joni Schwartz
This chapter addresses the challenges facing men of color who return to adult education after incarceration. It frames their experience as a war from a sociopolitical and cultural context, and then explains the support men need to succeed both in and outside the classroom.

8. Empty Promise: Black American Veterans and the New GI Bill 79
Alford H. Ottley
The 2008 GI Bill offers college funds for veterans. Yet Black male vets are not taking advantage of these benefits. This chapter examines personal and societal problems that hinder access to higher education for Black vets, and suggests some ways adult educators can advocate for these young men.

9. Black Males and Adult Education: A Call to Action 89
Brendaly Drayton, Dionne Rosser-Mims, Joni Schwartz, Talmadge C. Guy
In this concluding chapter, the editors offer their reflections on the key themes of this volume and implications for future research and practitioners of adult education.

INDEX 93

EDITORS' NOTES

Introduction

Imagine that you are swimming upstream against the current. What image or feeling comes to mind? The stronger the current, the more difficult it is to make any progress forward. The gentler the current, the less energy you have to exert to move ahead and yet, over time, swimming upstream drains you, exacts a toll on you, not just physically but also mentally, emotionally, and perhaps morally. As a metaphor, "swimming upstream" invokes the feeling of struggle, working harder than you should, and fighting against resistance or pressure to get where you want to be. It conveys the sense that your surroundings are working against you. We have used "swimming upstream" as a way for us to think about the experiences of Black males in American society, broadly, and in adult education, more specifically. The literature on marginalized populations covers a wide range of experiences in the field of adult education. This volume addresses a gap in that literature—that relating to Black males.

Black men are imaged in negative ways historically and contemporaneously. Facing a version of gendered racism, Black men, despite some highly visible examples to the contrary, are often defined by dominant narratives that present them as "at risk," "endangered," "pathological," "dangerous," and "immoral." The educational consequence of this stereotyping is that interventions focus on deficit-oriented strategies to "correct" the bad features of Black males rather than to acknowledge the historical and structural nature of gendered racism and its impact on the lives of Black men. Educational interventions that address only the individual conduct of Black men and avoid the structural dimensions of racism are poorly conceived and likely ineffectual.

This volume of *New Directions for Adult and Continuing Education* titled "Swimming Upstream: Black Males in Adult Education" is an introduction to salient topics and issues affecting Black males as they engage in adult basic education programs, pursue employment, and obtain higher education. It is grounded on the assumption that both the historical and current contexts of learning have a unique impact on the way in which these men participate in adult education. The chapter selections include academic research, theoretical discussions or literature summaries, as well as program descriptions and personal narratives with a concern for the "lived experiences" and the voices of Black men.

The editors are not exhaustive in covering the range of issues facing Black males in adult education. But we hope to challenge commonly held stereotypes, interactions, and polices. The volume is designed to raise questions about the unique experiences of this specific population and to explore the sociocultural dynamics that impact their education. Practitioners will be encouraged to reflect on their own practices as they work to engage Black males and other men of color in learning communities.

Several issues and themes emerged as we prepared this volume. First, early on it became clear to us that in adult education literature, unlike many other disciplines, little has been published to specifically address the Black male. This volume is an attempt to begin addressing this glaring omission. Second, we recognized an opportunity to challenge the "Black male narrative" prevalent in the educational, social, and political spheres, which positions the Black male as inherently deviant and destined for failure (Howard, 2013). Each contributor took deliberate steps to counter these notions by coupling their accounts of the systemic challenges Black males face with recommendations and solutions for support. Lastly, emergent from the chapters was the theme of *educational warfare* with all its incumbent emotional, physiological, and psychological ramifications. Utilizing this metaphor, the editors became increasingly aware that the struggle of racism in America often erupts in educational settings and that as adult educators, whether knowingly or unknowingly, we are all participants in the battle (Cuyjet, 2006; Hucks, 2011). One important purpose of this volume is to bring awareness to issues specific to Black males in adult education and to offer pedagogical strategies for engagement. From there, the choice falls on the adult educator's shoulders to determine what to do with this knowledge.

As the editors of this volume, we had the distinct pleasure of collaborating not only with each other but also with adult educators and students from a wide variety of experiences and perspectives, with expertise from adult basic education (ABE) to higher education.

Before we proceed to a brief overview of each chapter, one more word on our collaboration as editors of this project: Too infrequently, it seems, do we have the privilege of learning, engaging, and creating with colleagues with whom we share a strong sense of agency as well as deep respect and easy, honest communication. The editors of this volume had this fortunate collaborative opportunity.

Chapter Summaries

The opening chapter by Juanita Johnson-Bailey, Nichole Ray, and Tennille Lasker-Scott highlights the overarching issue of how racism and the intersecting forces in the United States differentially and with partiality affect the educational experiences of Black males by considering such factors as colorism, culture, and gender.

In Chapter 2, Talmadge C. Guy discusses the sociohistorical and deeply embedded myths that have dominated narratives about Black men and how these stereotypes shape the experience of professional Black men.

Brendaly Drayton, in Chapter 3, explores Black men's reasons for participating in an adult literacy program through the lens of gender identity. Chapter 4, by Joni Schwartz, extends the discussion of adult literacy to GED programs and describes how they serve as potential counter-space for African American and young men of color in response and opposition to previous negative school spaces.

Chapter 5 makes a strong argument that the presence and persistence of historical, systemic, and educational trauma is a new normal for young men of color and impacts their learning in all spheres of adult education. Authors Carlyle Van Thompson and Paul J. Schwartz include literary narrative and counterstories from a phenomenological study and documentary.

Dionne Rosser-Mims, Glenn A. Palmer, and Pamela Harroff in Chapter 6 specifically examine the Black male's reentry college experience and identify strategies to support their successful matriculation through college.

In Chapter 7, Brian Miller, Joserichsen Mondesir, Timothy Stater, and Joni Schwartz address the issue of Black males returning to adult education after incarceration. The authors frame the experience as a "war" from a sociopolitical and cultural context and explain what support Black men need to succeed both in and outside the classroom.

Chapter 8 focuses on the Black American vet. Alford H. Ottley offers an engaging discussion on these two fundamental questions: Are there deliberate and sustained institutional efforts to deny access to GI educational benefits to Black vets? Are there situational or societal barriers impeding access to educational benefits for Black vets?

In the closing chapter, the editors discuss implications for educators and areas for further research and writing in the field of adult education. This chapter highlights three key themes that formed the central connection to all chapters: critically reflective practice, culturally relevant pedagogy, and culturally relevant support services. We conclude this chapter with a call to action.

Acknowledgments

We would like to thank the authors for bringing their expertise, experiences, pain, struggle, and triumphs to their writing. A special thank you to the students who coauthored or informed the writing of the chapters; these men frequently challenged us to feel and think more deeply. Graduate assistant Hsiao-Hui Chen as well as Mardie McIlmoyl assisted in editing—thank you.

Dionne Rosser-Mims
Joni Schwartz
Brendaly Drayton
Talmadge C. Guy
Editors

References

Cuyjet, M. (Ed.). (2006). *African American men in college.* San Francisco, CA: Jossey-Bass.

Howard, T. C. (2013). *Black male(d). Perils and promise in the education of African American males.* New York, NY: Teachers College Press.

Hucks, D. C. (2011). New visions of collective achievement: The cross-generational schooling experiences of African American males. *The Journal of Negro Education, 80*(3), 339–357.

DIONNE ROSSER-MIMS *is an associate professor of adult education and assistant division chair of education at Troy University.*

JONI SCHWARTZ *is an associate professor in the Humanities Department at LaGuardia Community College, City University of New York.*

BRENDALY DRAYTON *earned her PhD in adult education from Pennsylvania State University.*

TALMADGE C. GUY *is an associate professor of adult education at The University of Georgia.*

1

This chapter explores the effects of historical and current racism on the educational experiences of American Black males. The authors use critical race theory to illustrate how assumptions about culture and gender have subverted the egalitarian ideals of adult education. Teachers and students are urged to use critical reflection and open discussion about racial issues.

Race, the Black Male, and Heterogeneous Racisms in Education

Juanita Johnson-Bailey, Nichole Ray, Tennille Lasker-Scott

The 2008 election of Barack Obama, a Black male, as the 44th president of the United States was a historic first that reignited a national conversation on race. The *Chronicle of Higher Education* posed in a bold headline, "Are We Living in a Post-Racial, Post-Ethnic America?" However, the national discussion that commenced was not on race, but specifically on the status of the Black American male. Despite the intensity and abundance of the questions around race and Black men, important underlying questions remained unaddressed. This chapter will undertake to answer a major query omitted from the intense race considerations: How do the complexities of race affect the dilemma of racial disparities?

Although race is a social construct that has no basis in biology (Frankenberg, 1993; Gregory & Sanjek, 1994; Omi & Winant, 1994), it consistently shapes lives and experiences. We are "raced" in our society, either consciously or not. Notwithstanding the assurances of anthropologists and biologists that there are no absolute racial categories, the accepted determinations of White, Black, Brown, and Yellow carry with them embedded and permanent stereotypes. Race and the social construct of race determine one's place in society. Racial classification designates a group's rights, privileges, or baggage (Frankenberg, 1993; McIntosh, 1995; Omi & Winant, 1994).

We bring to this discussion both firsthand experience and a theoretical understanding of race. We are mothers of an adult daughter and school-age male children; all of us live the daily reality of being Black in America. We are also researchers who employ a conceptual framework based on critical race theory (CRT), which posits that racism is an undeniable component of

American life (Bell, 1992; DuBois, 1903/1953; hooks, 1989; Outlaw, 1993). CRT values personal experience as a legitimate and appropriate basis for examination of racial subordination. Five tenets support the CRT perspective, as asserted by Ladson-Billings and Tate (1995): (a) a central focus on race and racism, (b) a direct and overt challenge to hegemonic discourse, (c) a commitment to social justice, (d) an honoring of the experiential base of marginalized people, and (e) a multifaceted disciplinary viewpoint. Our discussion in this chapter is steeped with an awareness of the diffusive nature of power and positionality (Foucault, 1980).

All areas of education reflect the world in which we live and are part of the systems that reproduce and maintain the whole of American society. Adult education, though founded on principles of leveling the playing field for all adults, especially those lacking a basic education (Cunningham, 1988; Johnson-Bailey, Baumgartner, & Bowles, 2010), does not stand in better stead than other fields. While the stated goal of adult education has been to empower learners so that they might engage in full citizenship, just the opposite often occurs. Adult education, like the other branches of American education, has followed the covert societal guidelines that have disenfranchised learners along racial and ethnic lines.

The Significance of Race in Education

Sixty years after the Supreme Court's 1954 *Brown v. Board of Education* public school desegregation decision, African Americans in the U.S. educational arena are still confined to a lesser existence, a legacy left behind by racist laws that forbade and then restricted their education with Jim Crow practices. Prejudice is not erased by law: Invisible systems and unspoken assumptions have created a hostile education system that still denies Blacks equal access.

At this point, we want to moderate our discussion by stating that any talk of race in America must examine the norm or concept of Whiteness (Keating, 1995). For although race is consistently presented as Black, Hispanic, or Asian, it is done so against the concealed specter of White as the norm. To label Whiteness and maleness as the norms of the culture accords power, against which all "others" are judged. We agree with Patai (1991) and Johnson-Bailey and Cervero (2000), who contend that such actions are intentional. The underlying ideas of Whiteness as superior and non-Whiteness as inferior or deficient are ever-present unless we attach the designation of racism.

In an educational setting, membership in a disenfranchised group translates into direct inequities: substandard education, tracking, and fewer opportunities for the future. Although we describe learners as at-risk or underprivileged, we do not refer to the inevitable and corresponding overprivileged student (Manglitz, Johnson-Bailey, & Cervero, 2005). It is a logical conclusion that the collective losses of the one group create the abundance of another.

Black Men and Education. An assessment of the state of American schooling readily reveals that African American males suffer from higher high school dropout rates and lower college entry and completion rates than any other racial or ethnic group. However, we contend that African American males are the proverbial canary in the educational mines, warning of dangers and pitfalls that are inherent in our educational system. Although race is a central location for the negotiation of power and privilege in education and in society, it is rarely coupled with a discussion of maleness unless the problem of the educational environment being researched is the African American male.

For clarification, let us briefly focus on Black males and the American educational system, looking explicitly at how African American males have fared inside of the compulsory elementary and high school education, and how they have fared in higher education and in adult education. Black males fall at the bottom of most indices regarding school success. Approximately 47–50% of Black male students fail to graduate from high school (Schott Foundation for Public Education, 2012), with urban areas, such as New York City, Philadelphia, Washington, DC, Detroit, Cleveland, and St. Louis, having failure rates as high as 60%. In fact, in all but 12 of the 50 states and the District of Columbia, Black males graduate at a lower percentage than Latino and White males and females, and also lower than Black females (Schott Foundation for Public Education, 2012).

Statistics are similar for higher education. Black college students experience issues that are exacerbated by racism. Sixty percent of Black students encountered racism (overt and covert forms) and routinely feel that there is bias in the ways that they are treated and graded (Allen, 1988; Engberg, 2004; Suarez-Balcazar, Orellana-Damacela, Portillo, Rowan, & Andrews-Guillen, 2003). Overall, undergraduate matriculation for Blacks with high school degrees who entered college in 2000 was 30.3%, with women at 35% of the total and men at 23% (Cose, 2003), making up 8.7% of all college students. However, the college graduation rate for 2000 showed that of the Blacks who completed college, Black women comprised 65.7% and Black men 34.2%, indicating a significant lack of completion for Black college men (NCES, 2002). However, what is lost in the statistics is that the percentage of Black students who attend four-year colleges and universities continues to be significantly smaller than their proportion in the population (Chen, 2005). Overall, Blacks are underrepresented by racial group membership in college. Though Black women are more successful in respect to their incidence in the four-year college participation and completion, it is only in comparison to Black males, who are the more unsuccessful.

The Crossroads of Heterogeneous Racisms. While we center on race for our chapter's discussion, we acknowledge that other important areas of disenfranchisement exist, such as gender, class, and physical ability. Therefore, let us begin this discussion by first troubling or deconstructing (Foucault, 1980) the notion of race, and then offering a gendered discussion of race. Racism is routinely researched as a distinct entity, but it is actually varied, often context-driven, and exists as an across-race and within-race phenomenon. In support of this position, we will offer accounts of how national origin, colorism, and gender all impact race.

An important first illustration is the use of and understanding of the word *Black* as a descriptor. For example, using the term "Black people" is a collective descriptive that represents persons of the African Diaspora, or anyone of African descent regardless of national origin or habitat. However, in reality, to be a Black African living on the continent of Africa or elsewhere in the world is different from being an African American residing in the United States. This variance is attributed to Africans having a culture connected to a prime homeplace (Okonofua, 2013; Omi & Winant, 1994; Waldinger, 2001). In "'I Am Blacker Than You': Theorizing Conflict Between African Immigrants and African Americans in the United States" (Okonofua, 2013), the author posits that Blacks from Africa and the Caribbean who reside in the United States see themselves differently because of their distinct culture and their perspective, which was developed in a homogenous society where they had majority status. This dissimilarity is also recognized by Whites and African Americans.

A second exemplification of this phenomenon is colorism among African Americans, a form of within-group racial discrimination, where lighter skin that is closer to Caucasian skin pigment is considered better, and an indicator of multiple superiorities. Although colorism is generalized as applicable to several disenfranchised groups of color in the United States (Asians, Hispanics, Blacks), there is significant literature only about Latinos and Blacks (Chavez-Dueñas, Adames, & Organista, 2014; Essed, 1996; Glenn, 2011; Russell, Wilson, & Hall, 1992). Skin color preference has been demonstrated in research on job applicants, customer partiality studies by advertisers, and longitudinal studies on socioeconomic measures in the African American population.

The final illustration for contemplation is the index of gendered racism (Essed, 1996), the intersection of two major forms of oppression: sexism and racism. According to Essed (1996), gendered racism is replete with master narratives driven by such forces as colonialism, sexual violence, economics, slavery, and politics, which are also major factors in the experiences of Black people. Gendered racism brings to the discussion of racism complex and separate legacies of inequities for men and women. When gendered racism pertains to Black women, it has been labeled as ethgender (Ransford & Miller, 1983) and also frequently referred to as double jeopardy (Beal, 1969/2008; Evans & Herr, 1991; King, 1988; Smith & Stewart, 1983).

Gendered racism is rarely thought of or acknowledged as affecting Black men. Additionally, members of the White race are set forth in history as the standard, and this depiction is most often accompanied by the phantom of maleness. Historically, when Whiteness and maleness are fused, they are viewed as the highest ideal of colonialism, the master, conqueror, and ruler (Alridge, 2006). In such an interpretation, the Black man and his male privilege are in a lesser position since the Black man's legacy is not one presented as part of the master narrative, and therefore a representation of the Black male is viewed in a lesser position. Although males, regardless of racial group membership, are privileged by their male gender, males of color, in this case Black males, are not part of the dominant ideology of history. Instead, a counternarrative is constructed for Black males that omits any place or importance that Black men have had in history (Alridge, 2006; Cox & Stromquist, 1998) and instead focuses on their physicality and sexuality, and consistently constructs a picture of Black men as pathologically flawed, with strong tendencies toward criminality and violence (Entman & Rojecki, 1992; Hines & Humez, 2002).

Black Males and Masculinity. What makes a man? How is masculinity constructed in the culture? In their important text on men and masculinity, *Men's Lives,* Kimmel and Messner (2013) assert that "To be a man is to participate in social life as a man, as a gendered being. Men are not born, they are made" (p. xvi). Normative masculinity requires that men be tough, independent, aggressive, unemotional, and the like. To be appropriately masculine, according to the dominant culture, men are to eschew any qualities such as nurturing, relationship, and sensitivity that are associated with femininity.

Behaviors and attitudes ascribed to manhood and masculinity are neither innate nor a biological imperative, but are social constructions legitimated by long-standing social, political, and economic institutions. Scholars of men's lives and masculinity have long asserted that men "make themselves" according to the social and cultural dictates of a particular point in time. For example, the "breadwinner/homemaker" model of the mid-20th century reinforces the popular belief that men should be the financial providers and that women are responsible for caregiving and labor in the home (Amott & Matthei, 1996). This model is rooted in beliefs that men and women are inherently different and, therefore, should be accorded certain tasks based on those differences. Individual men and women then perpetuate and uphold these beliefs that can result in separation and hierarchies created between them. Ultimately, these dualisms reinforce patriarchal and sexist systems in society.

Constructions of Black masculinity can also provide great insight into the impact of race in the educational experiences of Black men. There are a wealth of studies on Black males in P–12 education (Davis, 2003; Ferguson, 2000; Noguera, 2003) and higher education (Feagin, Vera, & Imam, 1996; Harper, 2006), but there are very few studies that examine the complex nature of Black masculinities and how they manifest within social institutions. However, researchers suggest that it is imperative that more studies be done on the gender identities of Black men, with a particular emphasis on the expressions of Black masculinity (Harris, Palmer, & Struve, 2011).

We suggest that in order to gain a more complex understanding of Black men in the educational system, it is beneficial to examine dominant constructions of Black masculinity. hooks (2004) uses the term "patriarchal masculinity" and posits, "In patriarchal culture, all males learn a role that restricts and confines. When race and class enter the picture along with patriarchy, Black males endure the worst impositions of gendered masculine patriarchal identity" (hooks, 2004, p. xii). If normative conceptions of masculinity state that to be a "real man" is to be tough, financial providers, aggressive, dominant, heterosexual, competitive, and other stereotypical traits, then where do Black men fit into this framework? How do race and racism factor into constructions of masculinity and the masculine charge to embody and enact said characteristics?

Black masculine identities, like all other identity markers, are formed by those who embody the identity, as well as by individuals outside of the group in question. Unfortunately, Black men are often viewed through stereotypical lenses constructed by the dominant culture and rooted in a history of racial insubordination (hooks, 2004). Violent, hypersexual, and lazy, for example, are three common stereotypical characteristics attributed to Black men. For instance, in her work on the politics of Black sexuality, Collins (2000) contends that the hypersexualization of Black men in films and music videos can have detrimental effects on Black men, as well as on Black women and children. The acceptance of Black masculine norms can be used either to perpetuate dominant notions of masculinity or to subvert hegemonic conceptions of masculinity. To illustrate, Majors and Billson's (1992) concept of the "cool pose" refers to particular ways of speaking, gestures, aesthetics, standing, walking, and the like that constitute expressions of Black masculinity. Black men have little or no institutional power and are often outside the bounds of acceptable masculine standards, so they engage in attitudes and actions such as cool pose as a way to empower themselves (Majors & Billson, 1992). It is a way of, as hooks (1989) puts it, "talking back" to particular constructions of manhood that are not applied to Black men.

The Relevance of Race to Educational Practice

Racism in its many forms has always been part of America's social system. However, education, another component of the great American system, is charged with improving the lives of its participants. We believe that when adult educators understand how racism affects the lived experiences of Black men, they will be able to create an educational environment that will empower all students. We suggest two means of ascertaining how race manifests in the experiences of Black male students. The first method is to conduct a cultural assessment of one's practice. The second approach is to consistently engage in critical reflection with learners.

When performing a cultural assessment of your educational practice, pose master questions that will allow you to examine how hidden and overt curricula function in your class. Ask if race/racism is appropriately part of a specific curriculum. Check to see if race is included in the readings and if the inclusion is analytical, judicious, and significant.

As pertains to the hidden curriculum, first determine whether Black men sign up for and subsequently participate in your classes. Because Black males are most often disenfranchised in the learning environment, their presence, participation in, or possible avoidance of your classes can indicate if perhaps your programs' classes are considered a safe space.

The second recommended approach in assessing the relevance of race is to engage in reciprocal critical reflection (Brookfield, 1990; Mezirow, 1990) on race with your Black learners. First, identify what assumptions regarding race are driving your thinking and actions and encourage your students to do the same. Next, in concert with your students, determine the validity of your assumptions, asking yourself how the knowledge on race and beliefs relate to your reality. Finally, integrate your new knowledge into your way of living and learning in order to make your environment empowering for its participants.

Conclusion

The impact of race and its related complexities regarding Black men are sensitive and difficult topics to deal with in the educational setting. However, it must be understood that race is present in our classrooms irrespective of the presence of people of color because the vestiges of race/racism occupy a space in all our classes. Therefore, the responsible choice dictated by the social justice core belief of our adult education field is to be egalitarian in our practice (Johnson-Bailey et al., 2010), which decrees not only that adult educators provide equal access and opportunities to their programs, but also that they critically examine the oppressive societal power systems such as racism. Additionally, such a position necessitates that within our educational setting we should work to promote environments that empower the learners, especially our Black males and other disenfranchised learners.

References

Allen, J. D. (1988). *Education of Blacks in the South, 1865–1930*. Chapel Hill: University of North Carolina.
Alridge, D. P. (2006). The limits of master narratives in history textbooks: An analysis of representations of Martin Luther King, Jr. *The Teachers College Record, 108*(4), 662–686.
Amott, T. L., & Matthei, J. A. (1996). *Race, gender and work: A multicultural economic history of women in the United States*. Boston, MA: South End Press.
Beal, F. M. (1969/2008). Black women's manifesto; double jeopardy: To be Black and female. *Third world women's alliance*. New York, NY: Random House. Retrieved from http://www.hartford-hwp.com/archives/45a/196.html
Bell, D. A., Jr. (1992). *Faces at the bottom of the well*. New York, NY: Basic Books.
Brookfield, S. D. (1990). Using critical incidents to explore learners' assumptions. In J. Mezirow (Ed.), *Fostering critical reflection in adulthood* (pp. 177–193). San Francisco, CA: Jossey-Bass.
Brown v. Board of Education, 347 U.S. 483 (1954).
Chavez-Dueñas, N. Y., Adames, H. Y., & Organista, K. C. (2014). Skin-color prejudice and within-group racial discrimination: Historical and current impact on Latino/a populations. *Hispanic Journal of Behavioral Sciences, 36*(1), 3–26.
Chen, X. (2005). *First-generation students in post-secondary education: A look at their college transcripts* (NCES 2005-171). U.S. Department of Education, National Center of

Education Statistics. Retrieved from http://nces.ed.gov/pubsearch/pubsinfo.asp?pubid=2005171

Collins, P. H. (2000). *Black feminist thought: Knowledge, consciousness and the politics of empowerment*. New York, NY: Routledge.

Cose, E. (2003). The Black gender gap. *Newsweek, 141*(9), 46–51.

Cox, J., & Stromquist, S. (Eds.). (1998). *Contesting the master narrative: Essays in social history*. Iowa City: University of Iowa Press.

Cunningham, P. M. (1988). The adult educator and social responsibility. In R. G. Brockett (Ed.), *Ethical issues in adult education* (pp. 133–145). New York, NY: Teachers College Press.

Davis, J. E. (2003). Early schooling and academic achievement of African American males. *Urban Education, 38*, 515–537.

DuBois, W. E. B. (1903/1953). *The souls of Black folk*. New York, NY: The New American Library.

Engberg, M. E. (2004). Improving intergroup relations in higher education: A critical examination of the influence of educational interventions on racial bias. *Review of Educational Research, 74*(4), 473–524.

Entman, R. M., & Rojecki, A. (1992). *The Black image in the White mind: Media and race in America*. Chicago, IL: The University of Chicago Press.

Essed, P. (1996). *Diversity: Gender, color, and culture*. Amherst: University of Massachusetts Press.

Evans, K. M., & Herr, E. L. (1991). The influence of racism and sexism in the career development of African American women. *Journal of Multicultural Counseling and Development, 19*(3), 130–135.

Feagin, J., Vera, H., & Imam, N. (1996). *The agony of education: Black students at White colleges and universities*. New York, NY: Routledge.

Ferguson, A. A. (2000). *Bad boys: Public schools in the making of Black masculinity*. Ann Arbor: University of Michigan Press.

Foucault, M. (1980). *Power/knowledge: Selected interviews and other writings, 1972–1977*. New York, NY: Pantheon.

Frankenberg, R. (1993). *White women, race matters: The social construction of Whiteness*. Minneapolis: University of Minnesota Press.

Glenn, W. J. (2011). A quantitative analysis of the increase in public school segregation in Delaware 1989–2006. *Urban Education, 46*(4), 719–740.

Gregory, S., & Sanjek, R. (1994). *Race*. New Brunswick, NJ: Rutgers University.

Harper, S. R. (2006). *Black male students at public universities in the U.S.: Status, trends and implications for policy and practice*. Washington, DC: Joint Center for Political and Economic Studies.

Harris, F., Palmer, R. T., & Struve, L. E. (2011). "Cool posing" on campus: A qualitative study of masculinities and gender expression among Black men at a private research institution. *Journal of Negro Education, 80*(1), 47–62.

Hines, G., & Humez, J. M. (2002). *Gender, race, and class in media*. Thousand Oaks, CA: Sage.

hooks, b. (1989). *Talking back: Thinking feminist, thinking Black*. Boston, MA: South End Press.

hooks, b. (2004). *We real cool: Black men and masculinity*. New York, NY: Routledge.

Johnson-Bailey, J., Baumgartner, L. M., & Bowles, T. A. (2010). Social justice in adult education: Laboring in the fields of reality and hope. In C. Kasworm, A. Rose, & J. Ross-Gordon (Eds.), *The handbook of adult and continuing education* (pp. 339–349). San Francisco, CA: Jossey-Bass.

Johnson-Bailey, J., & Cervero, R. M. (2000). The invisible politics of race in adult education. In A. L. Wilson & E. R. Hayes (Eds.), *Handbook of adult and continuing education* (pp. 147–160). San Francisco, CA: Jossey-Bass.

Keating, A. (1995). Interrogating "Whiteness," (de) constructing "race." *College English, 57*, 901–918.

Kimmel, M. S., & Messner, M. A. (2013). *Men's lives*. Upper Saddle River, NJ: Pearson.

King, D. K. (1988). Multiple jeopardy, multiple consciousness: The context of a Black feminist ideology. *Signs, 14*, 42–72.

Ladson-Billings, G., & Tate, W. F. (1995). Toward a critical race theory of education. *The Teachers College Record, 97*, 47–68.

Majors, R., & Billson, J. M. (1992). *Cool pose: The dilemmas of Black manhood in America*. New York, NY: Lexington Press.

Manglitz, E., Johnson-Bailey, J., & Cervero, R. (2005). Struggles of hope: How White adult educators challenge racism. *Teachers College Record, 107*(6), 1245–1274.

McIntosh, P. (1995). White privilege and male privilege: A personal account of coming to see correspondences through work in women's studies. In M. L. Andersen & P. H. Collins (Eds.), *Race, class, and gender: An anthology* (2nd ed., pp. 76–87). Belmont, CA: Wadsworth.

Mezirow, J. (1990). How critical reflection triggers transformative learning. In J. Mezirow (Ed.), *Fostering critical reflection in adulthood* (pp. 1–20). San Francisco, CA: Jossey-Bass.

National Center for Education Statistics, U.S. Department of Education (NCES). (2002). *Digest of Education Statistics 2001* (NCES 2002–130). Retrieved from http://nces.ed.gov/pubs2002/2002130.pdf

Noguera, P. A. (2003). The trouble with Black boys: The role and influence of environmental and cultural factors on the academic performance of African American males. *Urban Education, 389*, 341–459.

Okonofua, B. A. (2013). "I am Blacker than you": Theorizing conflict between African immigrants and African Americans in the United States. *SAGE Open, 3*(3), 1–14.

Omi, M., & Winant, H. (1994). *Racial formation in the United States: From the 1960s to the 1990s* (Revised ed.). New York, NY: Routledge.

Outlaw, F. H. (1993). Stress and coping: The influence of racism on the cognitive appraisal processing of African Americans. *Issues in Mental Health Nursing, 14*(4), 399–409.

Patai, D. (1991). U.S. academics and Third World women: Is ethical research possible? In S. B. Gluck & D. Patai (Eds.), *Women's words: The feminist practice of oral history* (pp. 137–153). New York, NY: Routledge.

Ransford, H. E., & Miller, J. (1983). Race, sex and feminist outlooks. *American Sociological Review, 48*, 46–59.

Russell, K., Wilson, M., & Hall, R. E. (1992). *The color complex: The politics of skin color among African Americans*. New York, NY: Random House LLC.

Schott Foundation for Public Education. (2012). *The urgency of now: The 2012 Schott 50 state report on public education and Black males*. Retrieved from http://blackboysreport.org

Smith, A., & Stewart, A. J. (1983). Approaches to studying racism and sexism in Black women's lives. *Journal of Social Issues, 39*(3), 1–15.

Suarez-Balcazar, Y., Orellana-Damacela, L., Portillo, N., Rowan, J. M., & Andrews-Guillen, C. (2003). Experiences of differential treatment among college students of color. *The Journal of Higher Education, 74*(4), 428–444.

Waldinger, R. D. (Ed.). (2001). *Strangers at the gates: New immigrants in urban America*. Berkeley: University of California Press.

JUANITA JOHNSON-BAILEY, *the director of the Institute for Women's Studies at the University of Georgia, is the Josiah Meigs Distinguished Teaching Professor for Adult Education and Women's Studies.*

NICHOLE RAY *is a lecturer for the Institute for Women's Studies at the University of Georgia and is adjunct faculty in the Adult Education Program and the Qualitative Research Program at the University of Georgia.*

TENNILLE LASKER-SCOTT, *a PhD candidate in the University of Georgia's Adult Education Program, is the recipient of The Irene and Curtis Ulmer Scholarship for Adult Education and a Southern Regional Education Board fellow.*

This chapter discusses the sociohistorical and deeply embedded myths and stereotypes that have dominated narratives about Black men and how these shape the educational and professional experiences of Black men.

The (End)angered Black Male Swimming Against the Current

Talmadge C. Guy

A few years ago a friend invited my son and me to join him and his family on a fishing trip to Alaska. The annual salmon run was scheduled to take place in a few weeks. Although I was unable to make the trip, the prospect excited me and I promised that I would try to do the trip in the future. The image of countless salmon struggling mightily upstream to reach the headwaters where they would breed and eventually complete the circle of life was awe inspiring. I have always been amazed at the struggle these fish endure, swimming against the current, jumping waterfalls, all risking death at the hands of predator threats—bears and eagles—who patiently wait to gorge themselves on the easy pickings. The salmon run is an apt analogy for comprehending the life environmental circumstances faced by Black men in America. The difficulties of life, some more and others less severe, faced by Black males create circumstances that circumscribe available choices for Black men to lead meaningful, constructive, and productive lives. It is against the current of racism that Black men must navigate the challenges, pitfalls, and traps of life to lead meaningful and productive lives.

In this chapter, I discuss the dominant narratives that have shaped the view of Black males in American society. These narratives comprise myths and stereotypes deeply embedded in the sociohistorical and racist narratives about the lives of Black men. Variously referred to as stock, dominant, or majoritarian narratives, these descriptions constitute a deep cultural reservoir of meanings and interpretations that shape the popular view of Black men. They serve as a cultural resource and memory to interpret the experiences of Black men seeking advancement in education and work. In considering these narratives and their impact, it is important to understand them as expressions of both racism and White male patriarchy. The concept of "Blackmen" (Cornileus, 2013; Mutua, 2006) is useful as a way to conceptualize how the particular identity position of Black men intersects with race and gender to condition the lives of Black men. In other words, Black male lives are shaped within interlocking systems of race and gender (Andersen & Collins, 2007). Although systems of race and gender evolve into new formations (Omi & Winant, 1994), neither the basic power relations nor the dominant narratives about Black males change appreciably across historical time.

The Historical Character of Dominant Racial Narratives About Black Men

As the idea of race crystallized into a set of social relations that privileged Whiteness, narratives that depicted Black male inferiority became deeply entrenched in American culture. By the 19th century, these narratives became expressions and rationalizations of a racist ideology and were commonly held by Whites even among abolitionists (Fredrickson, 1987). Dominant racial narratives were constituted in a way to depict Black people as subhuman and immoral. In the 19th century, racial narratives assumed that White superiority over Blacks was complete in every way—in mind, spirit, and body. Black men were represented as depraved sexual predators, mentally deficient, lazy, and cowardly, essentially lacking in any morally redeeming qualities (Wiegman, 2001).

As a consequence, miscegenation was considered a crime against nature, and many Black men were hanged for alleged sexual attacks on White women. Initially rationalized on the basis of pseudoscientific knowledge about the inferiority of Black physiology, dominant racial narratives about Blacks began also to assume a more religious character. Even as late as 1963, in the *Loving v. Virginia* supreme court case about the legality of an interracial marriage, the trial judge appealed to Biblical evidence stating that "the fact that [God] separated the races shows that he did not intend for the races to mix" (Newbeck, 2004, p. 144).

White racial thinking about Blacks was never composed of a static set of ideas. Dominant racial narratives, or stock stories, constantly evolved and shifted to adjust to new objective realities such as the end of slavery or the end of separate but equal. Nevertheless, evolving narratives rested upon a basic set of assumptions that depicted Black people as inferior. In the civil rights era of the 1950s and 1960s, dominant narratives of Blacks evolved to adjust to new conditions. White resistance to Black equality ebbed for a time as voting rights, equal housing, and antipoverty programs were set in place in the 1960s and early 1970s. White backlash began to surface in the late 1960s. President Nixon's 1968 campaign that called on the "silent" majority to speak loudly against government programs that aided Blacks and the poor was a clarion call to the large majority of Whites who were anxious about the changing political, social, educational, cultural, and economic landscape in which Black rights were asserted. President Reagan's portrayal of poor Blacks characterized by the image of the "welfare queen" or President Bush's invocation of Willie

Horton in the 1988 presidential campaign tapped into White fear and anxiety about Blacks.

The emergence of gangsta rap in the 1980s and 1990s served to reinforce popular cultural views of Black males as violent and crime prone against Whites. It mattered little that the actual facts revealed that the level of Black-on-Black crime was much greater than that of Black-on-White crime (Smith & Cooper, 2011). Facts based on objective reality did little to alleviate White suspicions about Black males as a malevolent threat that was grounded in long-held myths and prejudices. This historical overview is intended to provide a backdrop to the analysis of the dominant narratives that seek to define Black males today. One of these narratives, that of the endangered Black male, has emerged over the past 25 years.

Imagining Black Men: Endangered, At Risk, Invisible

In September of 2013, Mayors Michael Nutter of Philadelphia and Mitch Landrieu of New Orleans held a joint press conference at the National Press Club in Washington to declare that Black men were becoming an "endangered species." Decrying the lack of attention given to urban violence, the mayors appealed for action to address the systemic problems facing urban Black communities—poverty, crime, undereducation, and unemployment. The endangered species metaphor has been used for years to depict the condition of Black men (e.g., Taylor-Gibbs, 1988).

How ironic that Black males should be thought of as a species—an endangered species at that! But where are the special steps to preserve, protect, rejuvenate, and animate the talents, abilities, and potential of Black males? Public discourse is virtually silent on this. Neither educational nor economic public policy debates center on the conditions or problems faced by Black males. This silence is telling because it serves simultaneously to mask the real experiences of Black men while serving to preserve the image of Black men as responsible for their own circumstances. The Endangered Black Male narrative serves to highlight the current status of Black men while masking any real consideration of the racism that shapes their lives.

Education and Training. What, then, are the educational effects of the structural and environmental threats that condition the lives of Black males? Gavins (2009) overviews the historical legacy of racism and its impact on the educational achievement of Black males. He notes that since the civil rights reforms of the 1960s and 1970s, Black males advanced in educational achievement almost on par with African American women. As public commitment to affirmative action, antipoverty programs waned and urban employment contracted, Black males lost ground in educational achievement in the 1980s and 1990s. From 1940 to 2000, the data are clear that advancement in Black educational achievement was accelerating. Viewing the status of Black male educational and economic achievement in light of a longitudinal unidimensional analysis is misleading.

The Schott Foundation reports that the educational achievement gap is real when comparing Black males against virtually every other demographic cohort (Schott Foundation for Public Education, 2010). If educational attainment has any social significance, the persistent gap between Black males and other demographic groups documented in this and other government reports and studies indicates the extent to which Black males are marginalized within educational systems from elementary to postsecondary levels. As much as poverty and social class may play a part in education gap, the data are clear that young Black males are likely to fall behind their counterparts in virtually all areas of academic achievement (Schott Foundation for Public Education, 2010).

The experience of Black males in schooling is often predictive of their career success later in life. The story here is a dreary one that shows that Black males are most often consigned to special education services and labeled as "educable mentally retarded" or "trainable mentally retarded" or "developmentally delayed" (Howard, Flennaugh, & Terry, 2012). Fewer than 30% of Black males function at grade level in key skills of reading and writing by the high school years. School dropout rates often exceed 60% in many major metropolitan school systems (Schott Foundation for Public Education, 2010). Young Black males are less likely to enter gifted or exceptional educational programs in secondary school, more likely to be classified as educable mentally retarded, and more likely to drop out of high school (Schott Foundation for Public Education, 2010). According to the United States Department of Commerce, in 2012 85.9% of Black males held at least a high school diploma or equivalent, while 19.5% held at least a bachelor's degree; comparable figures for White males were 92.5% and 35.9%, respectively (U.S. Department of Labor, 2013). Sixteen percent of Black males hold college degrees as compared with 32% of White males (Schott Foundation for Public Education, 2010). These data indicate the profoundly troubling condition of Black males if we consider how important educational attainment is to improving life chances. In an increasingly knowledge-based economy, the lack of requisite academic skills effectively closes off opportunities that would otherwise be available.

And yet educational initiatives to address the Black male achievement gap are weak and insufficient to deal with the problem at its core. As Black males negotiate schools, they simultaneously navigate the whirlpools and rough waters of prejudice and bigotry, of violence and crime, and of hopelessness and despair. The statistics are too plentiful to summarize here and are addressed in other chapters in this volume. The silent politics of race (Johnson-Bailey & Cervero, 2000) work against any meaningful educational undertaking to address the issues faced by Black males in schooling. Suffice it to say that not enough attention is given to the educational plight of young Black males in terms of creative and generative solutions to the problems that contribute to the educational gap they experience.

Employment and Career. The employment data for Black males are no less concerning than the educational data. Unemployment and underemployment among Black males continue to be several times higher than for their White counterparts. In a study at the University of Wisconsin, Milwaukee, focused on Black male employment in 20 large U.S. metropolitan areas, the researcher found that "by 2010, barely more than half of Black males in their prime working years were employed compared to 85 percent almost forty years ago" (Levine, 2012, p. 3). The decline of Black male employment rates dropped precipitously between 1950 and 1990 when only 40% of Black males between 25 and 64 were employed (Quillian, 2002). These trends have not reversed. In fact, labor force participation itself has declined for Black males indicating that far too many have given up looking for work. By the beginning of the past decade, Black males had only worked about 2/3 as much as White or Latino males. A major reason is that available jobs have left the areas of urban centers where Blacks live (Holzer & Offner, 2004; Wilson, 1987). As a result, it has become more difficult to find gainful employment in large, urban communities, leaving residents to seek out opportunities available in the underground economy.

Other factors contribute to Black male underemployment and wage disparity in the job market even when education and background are accounted for. In a study of employers' hiring practices of Blacks, Moss and Tilly (1996) found that over half of managers and employers interviewed had negative views of Black males as employees. The negative views derived from perceptions and experiences grounded in peripheral activities and not directly as a result of interacting with Black males in the workplace (Moss & Tilly, 1996). These perceptions of Black males effectively align with dominant discourses about Black males as poor investments for employers. Moss and Tilly theorized that the employers' focus on "soft skills" is connected to impressions, perceptions, and attitudes held by White employers. These impressions are not factually related to whether Black males can actually perform the work needed. They are what Colin and Preciphs (1991) term "perceptual racism." In the next section, I discuss the paradox of Black male exceptionalism in light of the foregoing discussion of Black male marginalization in education and the workforce.

Black Male Exceptionalism and Postracialism

The names are familiar—Joe Louis, Jackie Robinson, Willie Mays, Roy Campanella, Bill Russell, Muhammad Ali, Jim Brown, Wilt Chamberlain, James Brown, Smokey Robinson, Nat King Cole, Snoop Dogg, Richard Pryor—and the list goes on. There are many Black athletes and celebrities who achieved national and even international renown. Perhaps not until the emergence of Michael Jordan as a mega star did Black athletes command not only popular acclaim but also multimillion dollar professional sports contracts as well as multimillions of dollars in sponsorships with companies to sell their products. Today, athletes and celebrities like LeBron James, Kobe Bryant, Jay-Z, Will Smith, Tiger Woods, Denzel Washington, Sean "Puffy" Combs, and Floyd

Mayweather are among a younger generation of widely known and recognized elite celebrities.

From the perspective of dominant White narratives about Black men, examples such as these serve to reinforce the idea that racism has largely been eliminated in American society. It no longer represents a serious deterrent to Black success. With the removal of the legal and institutional apparatus that sustain *de jure* racial segregation, a number of scholars and commentators now ponder a postracial era (Ambinder, 2009; Tesler & Sears, 2010). For example, it was virtually unthinkable, just a few years ago, that a Black man could be elected president of the United States once, let alone twice.

Academics such as William Julius Wilson and Dinesh D'Souza have argued that racism was no longer a significant problem in America. Wilson's (1978) sociological study *The Declining Significance of Race* and D'Souza's (1995) polemical *The End of Racism* were important milestones marking the shift in the public imagination about the eradication of racism in American society. These publications gave credence to the dominant narratives about Blacks in general, and Black males in particular. Any gap in achievement, whether educational or economic, is squarely a problem of poor morals, attitudes, discipline, and character.

From the perspective of postracialism, to be at the top of one's profession—once a dim hope for Black men—now seems within reach given the instant recognition and popularity of a Muhammad Ali or a Lebron James. To acknowledge and celebrate the accomplishment of men like these is a welcome occurrence. But it is vital to be wary of claims that promote a "postracial" era in which race has declining significance. The objective reality suggests otherwise. In spite of the growing number and high visibility of Black males with celebrity status, most Black men struggle daily with the burden imposed by racism.

There are two consequences that flow from this state of affairs. The fame and success of a small number of elite athletes and celebrities provide a rationale for educational policy makers, legislators, and decision makers to blame Black men for the problems they face. This dominant view holds that Black men are the *cause* of their own problems and, if they would simply change their attitudes and behaviors, they could improve their life chances. From the standpoint of educational policy and programs, this point of view is justification for providing, at best, compensatory programming to address any educational or equity gap. Sadly, there is a brooding silence when it comes to addressing the serious and profound environmental and structural problems that Black men face. The crisis of the endangered or "at-risk" Black man is an insufficient basis to develop policies or programs that support fundamental change that will help Black men succeed.

A second consequence is, ironically, an unfortunate overstatement of the possibility of becoming the next Jay-Z or Kobe Bryant. Young Black men are seduced by the lure of fame and fortune to think that almost anyone can enter the elite ranks of Black stardom. How ironic it is that so much Black manhood is frustrated in attempts to acquire success in whatever way possible. Despite the almost impossible odds, the desire to attain some level of respect appears to be the driving force for many young Black men who see few, if any, other pathways to success (Messner, 1989). Ironically, by pursuing an interest in sports or music or other position of celebrity, many young Black men opt out of more achievable goals. The dominant narrative of Black men, especially young Black men, as endangered and disconnected from mainstream society is thereby reinforced by the very actions of many young Black men.

Swimming Against the Current: The Black Male Counter Narrative

Despite the bleak picture painted thus far, there are many examples of Black men who are leading productive lives in successful careers and family life. Their stories bring to light the contradictions inherent in the dominant narratives about Black males. What we are left with are competing narratives of Black males in America. On the one hand, Black males are considered endangered and at risk. On the other hand, Black males have achieved in significant ways despite the barriers that exist. It is true that the relative proportions of Black males who are celebrities and have achieved the highest ranks of their fields are a fraction of the total population. Nevertheless, the narratives articulate the paradox: on the one hand, Black men can achieve and overcome any obstacle if they work hard, obey the rules, and get a good education. On the other hand, Black men are marginalized far more in comparison to other demographic groups in the population, so much so that they are considered an endangered species.

The achievement of Black males contrasts sharply with the discourse of the endangered Black male. This contradiction is reflected in the challenges faced by most Black males in achieving successful careers. It is grounded in a social system that structurally constrains the achievement of Black men. Cornileus (2010, 2013) argues that viewing Black men through the prism of race alone is insufficient to explain the challenges faced by Black males. She adopts the concept of "Blackmen" to argue that it is the combination of race and gender that places Black men in such jeopardy. Gendered racism creates a double jeopardy for Black males that influences how their careers develop differently from their White male counterparts and Black professional women.

Wingfield (2007) says that gender positions men and women differently such that racism and patriarchy affect Black men differently than Black women. In the context of the workplace this means that Black men do not enjoy male privilege in the same way or to the same extent as White males. Instead Black males' "male privilege" is altered, modified, and minimized as a result of incipient racism. Feminist researchers have explored how gendered racism affects Black women, but the individual as well as institutional and societal effects on Black males are specific to them in ways not experienced by Black women or White men. Wingfield concludes her study saying, focusing on "racism as a gendered phenomenon offers a more nuanced depiction of its impact on African Americans and a more intricate portrayal of their responses to it." (p. 210). Since the focus of this volume is on Black men, it must be said that Black men uniquely experience racism because of their gender. Gendered racism provides an important analytical tool for understanding how Black men experience systems of racial and gender oppression.

The empirical and theoretical literature in adult education that addresses the issue of race has grown tremendously over the past 25 years. From the New Directions sourcebook by Colin and Hayes (1994), *Confronting Racism and Sexism*, to the *Handbook of Race and Adult Education* (Sheared, Johnson-Bailey, Colin, Peterson, & Brookfield, 2010), the progress in understanding racism in the professional field has been significant and noteworthy. However, very few studies give voice to the experiences of Black males in the field. When Black males have an opportunity to speak frankly and openly about their educational and work experiences, a more distinctive and refined view of racism and patriarchy emerges. The stories of Black men contained in this volume represent a significant, if modest, effort to expand the conversation about racism and sexism in the field.

Implications for Practice

From the preceding discussion several implications can be identified to inform the practice of adult educators and trainers who work with Black males. Implications are taken in terms of professional development, curricular, pedagogical, and program design issues. First, the professional development programs should encourage practitioners to acknowledge the subtle effects of majoritarian narratives on the unconscious and hidden assumptions that adult educators hold about Black males. This entails an understanding of one's positionality and privilege and how these intersect with race and gender issues in the educational setting (Manglitz & Cervero, 2010; Sparks, 2002).

Second, curricula used in educational and training contexts should be culturally relevant and inclusive (Guy, 1999, 2007; Sealy-Ruiz, 2007). Ensuring that curriculum materials reflect the experiences and knowledge of Black males and do not contain various forms of bias (Guy, 2007) can send a strong message to Black male participants that they are valued and are considered capable of achievement. A third implication concerns the choice of pedagogical approach employed by adult education practitioners. Methods and strategies that "give voice" (Haddix & Sealy-Ruiz, 2012; Sealy-Ruiz, 2013; Sheared, 1999) to Black males open the ideological space (Cunningham, 1996) for the experiences and knowledge possessed by Black males that can be used as a resource for supporting learning and achievement (Howard et al., 2012).

Finally, the values and priorities of planners should be reflected in a way that sees Black male adult learners as subjects rather than objects (Sparks, 2002), as learners who also have something to contribute to the learning process rather than as empty vessels waiting to be filled (Freire, 1970). The design decisions made by adult educators to develop and organize programs for adult learners that include Black males must attend the historical and ideological baggage that Black males carry with them. Curriculum developers should address the psychological, psychocultural as well as structural dimensions of racism that shape the lives of Black men. Deficit-oriented program models result in inadequate solutions to problems faced by Black men (Howard et al., 2012; Kim & Hargrove, 2013). To ignore any of these suggestions tends to reproduce dominant narratives about the inability of Black males to succeed.

Closing Reflections on Gendered Racism and Black Males

Opening curricular and pedagogical space for Black men's voices to be heard, to speak their experiences, and to analyze and interpret their own lives suggests the following points. First, adult educators who seek to make a difference in the lives of Black men must acknowledge the nature of gendered racism that recognizes the unique positionality of Black men within the social system. The debates over appropriate adult education policy are most effective when they are grounded in the historical and structural dimensions of "gendered racism" that shape the lives of Black males (Cornileus, 2013). A derivative insight of the foregoing suggests that Black men's lives are not an additive calculation of marginalization by Blackness and privilege by maleness (Andersen & Collins, 2007; Howard et al., 2012). It is likely that Black men are marginalized on the basis of race and privileged *and* marginalized on the basis of gender. At present, how these factors are contextualized and interact is poorly understood. Clearly, more research is needed to understand the workings of race and gender in the lives of Black men. Finally, as the press conference of Mayors Nutter and Landrieu suggests, perhaps the most important conclusion to be made is that more attention must be given to the real-world circumstances faced by Black men, carefully avoiding the tendency to reduce these concerns to facile psychological characterizations of Black men as deficient.

These conclusions are all based on a rejection of educational theories and strategies that are grounded in a deficit model of education (Kim & Hargrove, 2013). Deficit-oriented education is grounded in a human capital orientation in which individuals are valued to the extent to which they are integrated into and contribute to the development and growth of existing institutions and social relations (Cunningham, 1996; Grant & Sleeter, 1998). From a humanistic perspective, the value and potential of all human beings should be considered of the highest priority in adult education programs. Yes, educational initiatives that address the psychological or psychocultural dimensions of racism are still important, yet they are incomplete and inadequate to create sustained structural transformation. Without attention to the broader sociohistorical and structural dimensions of oppression, adult education programs risk failure at serving the full range of Black males' learning.

References

Ambinder, M. (2009, January 1). Race over? *The Atlantic*. Retrieved from http://www.theatlantic.com/magazine/archive/2009/01/race-over/307215/

Andersen, M., & Collins, P. (2007). Why race, class, and gender still matter. In M. Andersen & P. Collins (Eds.), *Race, class and gender: An anthology* (6th ed., pp. 1–17). Belmont, CA: Thomson Wadsworth Publishing.

Colin, S., & Hayes, E. (Eds.). (1994). *New Directions for Adult and Continuing Education: No. 61. Confronting racism and sexism*. San Francisco, CA: Jossey-Bass.

Colin, S., & Preciphs, T. (1991). Perceptual patterns and the learning environment: Confronting White racism. In R. Hiemstra (Ed.), *New Directions for Adult and Continuing Education: No. 50. Creating environments for effective adult learning* (pp. 61–69). San Francisco, CA: Jossey-Bass.

Cornileus, T. H. (2010). *A critical examination of the impact of racism on the career development of African American professional men in corporate America* (Unpublished doctoral dissertation). The University of Georgia, Athens.

Cornileus, T. H. (2013). "I'm a Black man and I'm doing this job very well": How African American professional men negotiate the impact of racism on their career development. *Journal of African American Studies, 17*(4), 444–460.

Cunningham, P. (1996). Race, gender, class, and the practice of adult education in the United States. In P. Wangoola & F. Youngman (Eds.), *Towards a transformative political economy of adult education: Theoretical and practical challenges* (pp. 139–148). DeKalb, IL: LEPS Press.

D'Souza, D. (1995). *The end of racism: Principles for a multiracial society*. New York, NY: Free Press.

Fredrickson, G. (1987). *The Black image in the White mind: The debate on Afro-American character and destiny, 1817–1914*. Hanover, NH: Wesleyan University Press.

Freire, P. (1970). *Pedagogy of the oppressed*. New York, NY: Continuum Books.

Gavins, R. (2009). A historical overview of the barriers faced by Black American males in higher education. In H. Frierson, W. Pierson, & C. Wyche (Eds.), *Black American males in higher education: Diminishing proportions. Diversity in higher education* (Vol. 6, pp. 13–29). Bingley, UK: Emerald Group Publishing.

Grant, C. A., & Sleeter, C. E. (1998). *Turning on learning: Five approaches for multicultural teaching plans for race, class, gender, and disability* (2nd ed.). Upper Saddle River, NJ: Merrill.

Guy, T. C. (Ed.). (1999). *New Directions for Adult and Continuing Education: No. 82. Providing culturally relevant adult education: A challenge for the 21st century*. San Francisco, CA: Jossey-Bass.

Guy, T. C. (2007). Learning who we (and they) are: Popular culture as pedagogy. In E. Tisdell & P. Thompson (Eds.), *New Directions for Adult and Continuing Education: No. 115. Popular culture and entertainment media* (pp. 15–23). San Francisco, CA: Jossey-Bass.

Haddix, M., & Sealy-Ruiz, Y. (2012). Cultivating digital and popular literacies as empowering and emancipatory acts among urban youth. *Journal of Adolescent and Adult Literacy, 56*(3), 189–192.

Holzer, H., & Offner, P. (2004). The puzzle of Black male unemployment. *Public Interest, 154*, 74–84.

Howard, T., Flennaugh, T., & Terry, C. (2012). Black males, social imagery and the disruption of identities: Implications for research and teaching. *Educational Foundations, 26*(1/2), 85–93.

Johnson-Bailey, J., & Cervero, R. (2000). The invisible politics of race in adult education. In A. Wilson & E. Hayes (Eds.), *Handbook of adult and continuing education* (pp. 147–160). San Francisco, CA: Jossey-Bass.

Kim, E., & Hargrove, D. (2013). Deficient or resilient: A critical review of Black male academic success and persistence in higher education. *The Journal of Negro Education, 82*(3), 300–311.

Levine, M. V. (2012, January). *Race and male employment in the wake of the Great Recession: Black male employment rates in Milwaukee and the nation's largest metro areas, 2010.* Center for Economic Development, University of Wisconsin. Retrieved from http://www4.uwm.edu/ced/publications/black-employment_2012.pdf

Manglitz, E., & Cervero, R. (2010). Adult education and the problem of the color (power) line: Views from the Whiter side. In V. Sheared, J. Johnson-Bailey, S. Colin, S. Brookfield, & Associates (Eds.), *The handbook of race in adult education: A resource for dialogue on race* (pp. 133–144). San Francisco, CA: Jossey-Bass.

Messner, M. (1989). Masculinities and athletic careers. *Gender and Society, 3*(1), 71–88.

Moss, P., & Tilly, C. (1996). Soft skills and race: An investigation of Black men's employment problems. *Work & Occupations, 23*(3), 252–276.

Mutua, A. D. (Ed.). (2006). *Progressive Black masculinities.* New York, NY: Taylor & Francis Group.

Newbeck, P. (2004). *Virginia isn't always for lovers. Interracial marriage bans and the case of Richard and Mildred Loving.* Carbondale: Southern Illinois University Press.

Omi, M., & Winant, H. (1994). *Racial formation in the United States: 1960–1990* (2nd ed.). London, UK: Routledge.

Quillian, L. (2002). *The decline of male employment in low-income Black neighborhoods, 1950–1990: Space and industrial restructuring in an urban employment crisis.* Retrieved from University of Wisconsin, Institute for Research on Poverty website: http://www.irp.wisc.edu/publications/dps/pdfs/dp124802.pdf

Schott Foundation for Public Education. (2010). *Yes we can: The Schott 50 state report on public education and Black males.* New York, NY: Author. Retrieved from http://blackboysreport.org/bbr2010.pdf

Sealy-Ruiz, Y. (2007). Wrapping the curriculum around their lives: Using a culturally relevant curriculum with African American women adult learners. *Adult Education Quarterly, 58*(1), 44–60.

Sealy-Ruiz, Y. (2013). Building racial literacy in first-year composition. *Teaching English in the Two-Year College, 40*(4), 384–398.

Sheared, V. (1999). Giving voice: Inclusion of African American students' polyrhythmic realities in adult basic education. In T. C. Guy (Ed.), *New Directions for Adult and Continuing Education: No. 82. Providing culturally relevant adult education: A challenge for the 21st century* (pp. 33–48). San Francisco, CA: Jossey-Bass.

Sheared, V., Johnson-Bailey, J., Colin, S., III, Peterson, E., & Brookfield, S. (Eds.). (2010). *The handbook of race and adult education: A resource for dialogue on racism.* San Francisco, CA: Jossey-Bass.

Smith, E., & Cooper, A. (2011). *Homicide trends in the United States, 1980–2008.* United States Department of Justice. Retrieved from http://www.bjs.gov/content/pub/pdf/htus8008.pdf

Sparks, B. (2002). Adult literacy as cultural practice. In M. Alfred (Ed.), *New Directions for Adult and Continuing Education: No. 96. Learning and sociocultural contexts: Implications for adults community, and workplace education* (pp. 59–68). San Francisco, CA: Jossey-Bass.

Taylor-Gibbs, J. T. (1988). *Young, Black and male in America: An endangered species.* New York, NY: Auburn House.

Tesler, M., & Sears, D. (2010). *Obama's race: The 2008 election and the dream of a post-racial America.* Chicago, IL: University of Chicago Press.

U.S. Department of Labor. (2013). *Employment status of the civilian noninstitutional population by age, sex, and race.* Washington, DC: Bureau of Labor Statistics. Retrieved from http://www.bls.gov/cps/cpsaat03.htm

Wiegman, R. (2001). The anatomy of lynching. In D. Hine & E. Jenkins (Eds.), *A question of manhood: A reader in U.S. Black man's history and masculinity, Vol. 2: The 19th century, from emancipation to Jim Crow* (pp. 349–369). Bloomington: Indiana University Press.

Wilson, W. J. (1978). *The declining significance of race.* Chicago, IL: University of Chicago Press.

Wilson, W. J. (1987). *The truly disadvantaged: The inner city, the underclass, and public policy.* Chicago, IL: University of Chicago Press.

Wingfield, A. H. (2007). The modern mammy and the angry Black man. African American professionals' experiences with gendered racism in the workplace. *Race, Gender and Class, 14*(1/2), 196–212.

TALMADGE C. GUY is an associate professor of adult education at The University of Georgia.

> 3
>
> *This chapter explores Black men's reasons for participating in an adult basic education and literacy program through the lens of gender identity.*

The Good Provider: Missing or Overlooked?

Brendaly Drayton

While there has been a growing body of literature on the "good mother" discourse in adult education (Prins & Willson-Toso, 2008), there has been little if any discussion of the other side of the coin: the "good provider" (Christensen & Palkovitz, 2001). Feminist research has shown the social expectation that mothers bear primary responsibility for the educational development of their children influences their decisions concerning higher educational pursuits (Luttrell, 1996). In contrast, there are discussions of men seeking higher levels of education for better jobs, but little exploration of the inspiration behind their goals. Notably, Gadsden, Wortham, and Turner's (2003) collaborative work on young urban Black men has shown that the hope of being a good father ranks high among their reasons for acquiring a General Education Diploma (GED®) and for seeking better employment options despite the many obstacles they faced. Anderson, Anderson, Friedrich, and Kim (2010) found in their review of adult and family literacy programs that the mothering discourse overlooked the importance of other family members' contributions to children's literacy development.

Drawing upon Gee's (2011) description of discourses as *"ways of recognizing and being recognized* as certain sorts of whos [sic] doing certain sorts of whats [sic]" (p. 178), the good provider is the husband and father whose work results in the needed resources for his family. Research on the good provider role affirms that it continues to be significant in how men evaluate and validate themselves in light of society's expectations of them as workers, fathers, and husbands (Christensen & Palkovitz, 2001; Roy, 2004). Therefore, failure to examine the influence of the good provider discourse limits our understanding of the role gender plays in adult education. I utilize the findings of a qualitative case study of six Black men in an adult basic education and literacy (ABEL) program (Drayton, 2012) to encourage reflection on how these men's aspirations and goals might inform adult educator perspectives and program approaches. Analysis of in-depth interviews and observational data indicates that the participants in this study utilized the ABEL program as a resource for enacting their perceptions of manhood and paternal provision.

My framework for this discussion combines a social practices view of literacy, gender as performance, and Black men's conceptions of manhood. A social practices view of literacy (Barton & Hamilton, 2000; Street, 1984) recognizes that access to, engagement with, and outcomes of literacy are underpinned by values, power relationships, and learner agency framed within a social, historical, and economic context. The concept of gender as performance (Butler, 1988) asserts that the acting out of socially sanctioned beliefs and behaviors validates and strengthens our perceptions of gendered roles. Identity is a relational concept; therefore, it is not surprising that in Hunter and Davis's (1994) study of Black men's conceptions of manhood, they found that the "central challenge of manhood was defined in terms of what they expected of themselves" (p. 29). Such expectations were shaped by family role, individual perspective on identity, self-development, connections to family and community, spirituality, and worldview. Hammond and Mattis (2005) build on this finding by identifying categories of manhood that I will use to describe the men's conceptions of manhood. I will begin by reviewing the good provider role, then present findings of the study, and conclude with a discussion of implications for adult education.

Literature Review

The centrality of the good provider or breadwinner role is strengthened by its attachment to various social positions such as father, husband, and worker (Christensen & Palkovitz, 2001). The advent of the industrial revolution restructured the perception and enactment of gendered identities so that women were connected to work within the home and excluded from independent provision, while men were connected to work outside the home and assigned the provider role (Bernard, 1981). Consequently, meeting the social expectations of being a good mother and a good provider became integral parts of women's and men's identities, respectively. Today, despite women's increased presence in the workplace and two-earner families, society still holds men accountable to this role, making a distinction between earning money and providing (Loscocco & Spitze, 2007).

Recent scholarship on fathering has expanded the view of fathers' involvement to include meeting the educational, emotional, physical, and spiritual needs of their children (Christensen & Palkovitz, 2001; Roy, 2004). In Forste, Bartowski, and Jackson's (2009) study, low-income men cited the importance of "being there" for their children. "Being there" meant providing for their children's needs as nurturer, teacher, and protector. The dominance of the good provider discourse in measuring the good father by earning capacity devalues the nurturing component of fathering. The "good provider" definition reduces socially sanctioned options for men with limited economic resources to gain respect through other types of provision. Many of the men in ABEL programs are either unemployed or work sporadically.

The Race Factor. Struggle is central to the concept of Black manhood because of the social and economic consequences of race relations in the United States (Jackson & Dangerfield, 2004). In her historical overview of families of color in the United States, Dill (1999) pointed out that race has been used as a basis for denying legal, social, and economic support to Black families. Ensuing stressors required alternate strategies to sustain family survival. For Black men, White male dominance was perpetrated through castration, rape of their wives, sale of their children, and other forms of dehumanizing treatment that attacked, suppressed, and vitiated their roles as providers and protectors of their families. Following emancipation, Black men were held to the hegemonic construction of the good provider role. At the same time, the legacy of slavery and systemic discriminatory practices denied them economic opportunities to adequately provide for their families. This phenomenon is captured by the analogy of the salmon swimming upstream, as described in Chapter 2. Consequently, concepts of Black manhood cannot be captured under general ideas of power and privilege associated with White men, because the experience of racial oppression imbues Black men's concepts of manhood with the components of struggle and the desire for self-authorship, achievement, and community recognition (Jackson & Dangerfield, 2004).

The Class Factor. Daily concerns about meeting basic family needs foster preoccupation with the provider role among working-class men. For example, Watkins, Walker, and Griffith's (2010) meta-analysis of qualitative studies on Black men's mental health showed that, in contrast to middle-class men, those of low economic circumstance experienced higher stress levels and were concerned with issues such as crime and drug infestation, health issues, and housing. There are many factors such as low educational attainment, lack of economic social networks, and discrimination that contribute to the high incidence of low-wage jobs, sporadic employment, and unemployment among low-income Black men (Anderson, 2008; Jarrett, Roy, & Burton, 2002; Royster, 2003). These conditions reflect the experiences of the men in this study.

Much attention has been focused on Black men's absence from the home as the cause of persistent family poverty, and as a result of the reproach and shame associated with failure to meet society's expectations of the good provider (Christensen & Palkovitz, 2001). In recognizing the many challenges faced by low-income Black men, Roy (2005) insightfully notes, "With ambiguity about how to achieve respect and success in the traditional package deal, men are at great risk for not only becoming unknown workers but unknown partners and parents as well" (p. 96). This chapter seeks to disrupt the prevailing stereotype of the bad provider by analyzing the purposes and goals of men in an ABEL program, and by drawing attention to these unknown workers, partners, and parents.

Research Design

The study took place at an ABEL site in a large northeastern city. I used a qualitative multicase study (Stake, 2005) of six men between the ages of 21 and 64 to explore how Black men made sense of their literacy experiences. Criterion and purposive sampling (Patton, 2002) was effective in recruiting participants from the target group. Data were collected over a period of three months through 16 interviews and 19 hours of participant observations. On average, the interviews were an hour in length and were tape-recorded and transcribed. I used narrative analysis, specifically Riessman's (2008) performance/dialogic approach, as my interpretive and analytic lens. This was helpful in discerning how the men connected particular meanings to their experiences. Also, the analysis identified social, cultural, and institutional factors that informed the men's narratives. Discussion of the findings of the study will focus on the four men who held paternal responsibilities: Roddy Rod (age 64), Raymond (age 56), Ice (age 55), and Junior (age 38). The names used are participant-chosen aliases.

Findings of the Study

The men connected participation in the ABEL program to their roles as adults, fathers, grandfathers, and sons. Employment was the most frequently cited reason for learning to read or getting a GED®. Getting employment with the ability for promotion was a means of acting out their perceptions of manhood through providing economic resources for themselves and their families. In terms of self, the men spoke of independence and self-authorship. Concerning their roles as fathers, grandfathers, and sons, they spoke of responsibility.

Independence. The men's narratives show that they expected increased independence as an outcome of participation in the program, albeit different types of independence. The men sought freedom from having to rely on "dead end" jobs without possibility of advancement or medical coverage. Three of the men told stories of how their low literacy skills or lack of a GED® impeded their advancement to better-paying positions. For instance, Junior stated, "If you are trying to better yourself and you want an extra promotion, and if you don't have it [GED® or high school diploma] then it's a tough break" because you are "stuck" making about $27,000 a year instead of $60,000 a year. Junior also showed the symbolic meaning attached to the GED® when he declared that he could be "proud" and tell the employers he had one when it was requested.

Similarly, Raymond, who had a third-grade reading level, recognized that economic independence was contingent upon educational accomplishment. He explained that he was "pushing real hard" to learn to read because his low literacy skills hindered employment. Raymond also sought independence from relying on his family, friends, and strangers to fill out applications for him. He declared: "That's something I should be doing." He echoed the reproach he felt from society and the resulting shame: "[They say], you know that boy, he 56 years old and don't know how to read and write. What the hell wrong with 'im? I understand that." Raymond often compared himself to children who could read. His narratives show that his low literacy skills violated his concept of manhood because others had to take on his responsibilities as a self-sufficient adult. Autonomy was the second most referenced category in Hammond and Mattis's (2005) study; it is defined as "having power, control, or authority over the choices and decisions related to one's life as well as being self-sufficient, free governing, and able to express one's uniqueness" (p. 120).

Manhood is covalidated by the community (Jackson & Dangerfield, 2004). Therefore, the men's narratives reflected the importance of achievement or its lack. Growth and maturity as well as respect were ranked among the top 10 categories in Hammond and Mattis's (2005) study. These two categories are linked because the men's failure to meet their own and society's expectations of self-development resulted in shame. The society in which we live greatly influences what we value, the measures we use to determine what is good or bad, and how we view ourselves (Gee, 2011). In the context of a literate society, the men recognized that their ability to provide for themselves and their families and to earn respect was mediated by a rite of passage marked by educational level and the minimum accreditation of a high school diploma or GED®.

Responsibility to Family. Most of the men framed their desire for economic and educational independence around their roles as fathers, grandfathers, and adult sons. This aligned with Hammond and Mattis's (2005) study, in which responsibility–accountability was the most referenced category. It is described as "taking, handling, or being aware of one's responsibility to oneself, family, and others" and as "being accountable for one's actions, thoughts, and behaviors" (p. 120). Notably, 6 of the 15 categories were directly connected to an individual's contributions to family and community: providing and waymaking ("being a provider for oneself, family, or other" [p. 120]), family centeredness, leadership–guidance, protecting family–others, and emotional connectedness. These categories were evident in the men's discussions of their aspirations for participating in and completing the program.

Some of the narratives gave insight into the psychological stress the men brought into the learning environment. At the time of the interview, Roddy Rod was attending his third adult education program at the age of 64 for the sole purpose of self-improvement. However, he explained that the impetus for attending his first GED® program was his responsibility as a young father and husband at the age of 19. He described the emotional and psychological stress he felt about fulfilling those roles with low literacy skills:

> It really wasn't easy. Very scary, very, you know, unsure of myself a lot of times saying, 'Wow, how am I going to do this? How am I going to manage? How am I going to take care of children?'

As he explained, a father's "goal is to do the best that he can for his family, better than his parents did for him." Nevertheless, Roddy Rod dropped out of that program after nine months because he considered it "such a big waste" of time.

The staff had placed him in the wrong class and refused to let him take the scheduled test despite his request. Roddy Rod wanted to take the test to see how much progress he had made. He had no proof that skill development (benefit) outweighed the time and energy (cost) invested in the program (Beder, 1991). Consequently, Roddy Rod invested his time and energy in working multiple jobs to provide for his family. Upon reflection, he affirmed that, despite his low literacy skills, he had provided for his family better than his parents had provided for him. Roddy Rod's portrayal of himself accords with the categories of surviving–overcoming and providing–waymaking.

Although experiences of surviving and overcoming were evident in all the men's narratives, some of the men faced obstacles that hindered their characterization of themselves as provider–waymaker for their children and grandchildren. Junior, for example, hoped to get custody of his youngest son because he believed that the mother's frequent residential moves negatively affected his son's academic progress: "So now she's like moving from place to place with my son. So that's the reason why I was stepping in." This situation was a replay of Junior's early schooling experiences; he believed that parental moves had contributed to his slow academic progress. However, Junior was out of work at the time of the interview and worked sporadically. His prior felonies limited options for job placement, and those work hours often conflicted with adult education program schedules, delaying the acquisition of his GED®. Ex-offenders are expected to meet parental obligations, but their ability to find work is constrained by discriminatory practices and laws that restrict the types of jobs they can hold (Pager, 2008). Consequently, addressing the needs of his son, as he perceived them, hinged on Junior's finding stable employment. The men's stories demonstrate the challenge many low-income men face in finding jobs and the dilemma of taking available jobs versus completing ABEL programs.

Three of the men expanded the narrow focus on economics to include knowledge as a dimension of provision. As adult sons, fathers, and grandfathers, they felt it was their responsibility to provide knowledge and wisdom. The men's narratives draw attention to the three-generational family structure in their understanding of family roles and responsibilities. Two of the men included their mothers as beneficiaries of their efforts. For example, Ice explained his program goals and aspirations this way: "To read. Get my GED® and start to keep money in the bank for my kids, my mother, and everything, 'cause I got a lotta brothers." He added that his brothers were on drugs and not providing for his mother. Ice had overcome drug addiction and gained custody of his children. At the time of the interview, he was on disability because of a back injury.

Two of the men were learning how to read so that they could read to their grandchildren and answer their questions. Raymond, who had taken on the fathering responsibilities for his granddaughter, related his response when his granddaughter asked him to read to her: "I sat on the couch and I cried because I couldn't—I didn't know how. She asked why I was crying so I had to sit there and tell her the truth: Grandad don't know how to read." Although Raymond provided financial support, attended parent–teacher meetings, and actively encouraged his granddaughter to do well in school, he was particularly burdened by his inability, as he saw it, to provide "knowledge" and "wisdom" to his children. In Black families, grandparents have held, and continue to hold, an important role in passing on cultural values and beliefs (Bullock, 2007; Hunter & Taylor, 1998). In our literate society, parents are expected to employ literate practices in the home that will facilitate early educational success for their children (Prins & Willson-Toso, 2008). Low literacy skills detract from the fulfillment of that role.

In sum, the men attended the ABEL program to fulfill the expectations of the good provider role as fathers, grandfathers, and adult sons. The men's narratives problematize the stereotype of the uninvolved, unproductive, predatory low-income Black male. Their stories convey that many challenges mediate between aspirations and behaviors. The increased importance of literacy in the men's daily lives enhanced their desire to learn to read and acquire a GED®. As Brandt (2003) pointed out, literacy learning is motivated by technological and social change, not just by individual choice. Personal choice, however, determines how that learning will be used. Literacy as a social practice was intricately connected to the men's gendered identities. Literacy development and acquisition of the GED® were ways for the men to exert control over their lives, to provide for themselves and others, and to gain respect.

Implications for Practice

The men's narratives offer some areas of consideration for adult educators. They indicate that the creation of a supportive learning environment requires an understanding of the lived experiences of low-income undereducated Black men. First, widely accepted identity models shape how we perceive and interact with others and interpret particular behaviors (Neal, McCray, Webb-Johnson, & Bridgest, 2003; Wortham, 2006); therefore, as adult educators we need to examine how negative Black male stereotypes inform student–teacher interaction and program policy. For example, program planners should be familiar with factors that contribute to inconsistent attendance rather than assuming learners' disinterest or lack of commitment. A flexible GED® program might include less-restrictive attendance policies and incorporate some form of distance learning.

Second, the men's narratives stress that respect as a conceptual component of manhood has a high salience for low-income Black men. In our society, Black males are routinely subjected to slights, indignities, and unfair treatment by systems of authority. The ideal learning environment would engage them as valued human beings (Huo & Binning, 2008). Educators convey respect when they solicit learners' perspectives and experiences as resources for learning. The classroom environment promotes equity when men feel welcomed and their voices heard. In addition, expressing concern for the men's well-being and following up when they are absent promote a sense of belonging and trust.

Third, the men's aspirations demonstrate a need for programs to provide support for Black men's multiple roles and identities. Life-stage roles and events inspire learning goals beyond employment. The growing discourse of fathers as nurturers and the centrality of the good provider role to men's self-concept raise questions about overlooked needs. The expectation of being a waymaker may prohibit some men from disclosing the challenges they face and seeking help. The narrow emphasis on employment places men who face limited economic resources and structural obstacles in a "no-win situation" (Cornwall, 1997) that reminds them of their failure. Programs might be more supportive by including the nurturing components of fathering in text and language, as well as in parenting classes. Text, image, and language are powerful mediums that convey which identities are socially sanctioned (Anderson, Streelasky, & Anderson, 2007). Programs can support educators by providing tools and strategies that will help them meet the needs of this population.

Finally, it is important that instructors be intentional about discussing the benefits of participation and completion of goals. The responsibilities of paternal provision are very stressful for low-income Black men. The demands of the good provider role are especially heavy on ex-offenders, whose identities limit job options, raising questions about the benefit of a GED® for employment. In other words, we must explicitly convey that literacy and GED® courses will improve learners' ability to meet daily needs. Making space for Black men's multiple roles and identities can promote engagement by building stronger connections between aspirations, learning goals, and program offerings. Connection begins with open discussions that allow the men's needs to be heard and addressed. Envision them as members of families and communities who strive to be good providers, though encumbered by limited resources and many obstacles. Good providers among low-income Black men are not missing, they are overlooked!

Acknowledgments

I am grateful to the participants for sharing their experiences and the Africana Research Center for funding the project.

References

Anderson, E. (2008). Against the wall: Poor, young, Black and male. In E. Anderson (Ed.), *Against the wall: Poor, young, Black and male* (pp. 1–27). Philadelphia: University of Pennsylvania Press.

Anderson, J., Anderson, A., Friedrich, N., & Kim, J. E. (2010). Taking stock of family literacy: Some contemporary perspectives. *Journal of Early Childhood Literacy, 10*(1), 33–53.
Anderson, J., Streelasky, J., & Anderson, T. (2007). Representing and promoting family literacy on the World Wide Web: A critical analysis. *The Alberta Journal of Educational Research, 53*(2), 143–156.
Barton, D., & Hamilton, M. (2000). Literacy practices. In D. Barton, M. Hamilton, & R. Ivanic (Eds.), *Situated literacies: Reading and writing in context* (pp. 7–34). New York, NY: Routledge.
Beder, H. (1991). *Adult literacy: Issues in policy and practice*. Malabar, FL: Krieger.
Bernard, J. (1981). The good-provider role: Its rise and fall. *American Psychologist, 36*(1), 1–12.
Brandt, D. (2003). Changing literacy. *Teachers College Record, 105*(2), 245–260.
Bullock, L. (2007). Grandfathers raising grandchildren: An exploration of African-American kinship networks. *Journal of Health and Social Policy, 22*(3/4), 181–197.
Butler, J. (1988). Performative acts and gender constitution: An essay in phenomenology and feminist theory. *Theatre Journal, 40*(4), 519–531.
Christensen, S. L., & Palkovitz, R. (2001). Why the "good provider" role still matters: Providing as a form of paternal involvement. *Journal of Family Issues, 22*(1), 84–106.
Cornwall, A. (1997). Men, masculinity and "gender in development." *Gender and Development, 5*(2), 8–13.
Dill, B. T. (1999). Fictive kin, paper sons, and compadrazgo: Women of color and the struggle for family survival. In S. Coontz, M. Parson, & G. Raley (Eds.), *American families* (pp. 2–19). New York, NY: Routledge.
Drayton, B. (2012). *Literacy and identity: Reflections of six African-American males in an adult literacy program* (Doctoral dissertation). Available from ProQuest Dissertations and Theses database. (UMI No. 3654656)
Forste, R., Bartowski, J., & Jackson, R. (2009). "Just be there for them": Perceptions of fathering among single low-income men. *Fathering, 7*(1), 49–69.
Gadsden, V., Wortham, S., & Turner, H. M., III. (2003). Situated identities of young, Black fathers in low-income urban settings [Electronic Version]. *Family Court Review, 41,* 381–399.
Gee, J. P. (2011). *How to do discourse analysis: A toolkit.* New York, NY: Routledge.
Hammond, W. P., & Mattis, J. S. (2005). Being a man about it: Manhood meaning among Black men [Electronic Version]. *Psychology of Men & Masculinity, 6,* 114–126.
Hunter, A., & Davis, J. E. (1994). Hidden voices of Black men: The meaning, structure, and complexity of manhood. *Journal of Black Studies, 25*(1), 20–40.
Hunter, A., & Taylor, R. (1998). Grandparenthood in African American families. In M. Szinovacz (Ed.), *Handbook on grandparenthood* (pp. 70–86). Westport, CT: Greenwood Press.
Huo, Y., & Binning, K. (2008). Why the psychological experience of respect matters in group life: An integrative account. *Social and Personality Psychology Compass, 2*(4), 1570–1585.
Jackson, R. L., II, & Dangerfield, C. L. (2004). Defining Black masculinity as cultural property: Toward an identity negotiation paradigm. In R. L. Jackson II (Ed.), *Black communication & identities: Essential readings* (pp. 197–208). Thousand Oaks, CA: Sage.
Jarrett, R., Roy, K. M., & Burton, L. (2002). Fathers in the "Hood": Insights from qualitative research on low-income African-American men. In C. S. Tamis-LeMonda & N. Cabrera (Eds.), *Handbook of fatherhood involvement* (pp. 211–248). Mahwah, NJ: Lawrence Erlbaum Associates.
Loscocco, K., & Spitze, G. (2007). Gender patterns in provider role attitude and behavior. *Journal of Family Issues, 28*(7), 934–954.

Luttrell, W. (1996). Taking care of literacy one feminist's critique. *Educational Policy, 10*(3), 342–365.
Neal, L., McCray, A., Webb-Johnson, G., & Bridgest, S. (2003). The effects of African American movement styles on teachers' perceptions and reactions. *The Journal of Special Education, 37*(1), 49–57.
Pager, D. (2008). Blacklisted: Hiring discrimination in an era of mass incarceration. In E. Anderson (Ed.), *Against the wall: Poor, young, Black, and male* (pp. 71–86). Philadelphia: University of Pennsylvania Press.
Patton, M. Q. (2002). *Qualitative evaluation and research methods* (3rd ed.). Newbury Park, CA: Sage.
Prins, E., & Willson-Toso, B. (2008). Defining and measuring parenting for educational success: A critical discourse analysis of the parent education profile. *American Educational Research Journal, 45*(3), 555–596.
Riessman, C. (2008). *Narrative methods for the human sciences.* Los Angeles, CA: Sage.
Roy, K. M. (2004). You can't eat love: Constructing provider role expectations for low-income and working class fathers. *Fathering, 2*(3), 1–21.
Roy, K. M. (2005). Transitions on the margins of work and family life for low-income African American fathers. *Journal of Family and Economic Issues, 26*(1), 77–100.
Royster, D. A. (2003). *Race and the invisible hand.* Los Angeles: University of California Press.
Stake, R. (2005). Qualitative case studies. In N. Denzin & Y. Lincoln (Eds.), *The Sage handbook of qualitative research* (3rd ed., pp. 443–466). Thousand Oaks, CA: Sage.
Street, B. (1984). *Literacy in theory and practice.* New York, NY: Cambridge University Press.
Watkins, D., Walker, R., & Griffith, D. (2010). A meta-study of Black male mental health and well-being. *Journal of Black Psychology, 36*(3), 303–330.
Wortham, S. (2006). *Learning identity.* New York, NY: Cambridge University Press.

BRENDALY DRAYTON earned her PhD in adult education from Pennsylvania State University.

4

> This chapter is based on the findings of an ethnographic study of an urban General Education Development (GED®) program and suggests that, for some marginalized African American and other young men of color, adult education programs are counter-spaces (Yosso, Ceja, Smith, & Solorzano, 2009) of spatial justice in opposition to previous negative school spaces. The chapter is framed from the perspective of critical race theory.

High School Equivalency as Counter-Space

Joni Schwartz

General Education Development (GED®) preparation courses and other alternative high school equivalency (HSE) examinations, HiSET®—High School Equivalency Test and the TASC®—Test Assessing Secondary Completion, continue to be a significant focus of adult basic education (ABE) in the United States. This is despite efforts to retain students in high school and the 2014 redesign of the GED® test. For many marginalized African American males and other young men of color who have not had the privilege of attending a quality high school, HSE or GED® programs are reasonable alternatives to high school completion (Tuck & Neofotistos, 2013). Collectively, African American and Hispanic men are the least likely to graduate from high school or college, and according to recommendations from a recent national report, "policymakers must make improving outcomes for young men of color a national priority" (College Board Advocacy & Policy Center, 2013, p. 70).

While policymakers hopefully work to make systemic changes to address racial inequities that have historically haunted public and higher education, African American and other young men of color are entering adult education for HSE preparation. In fact, during the 1990s, there was an actual "adolescentizing" of the GED® (Rachal & Bingham, 2004, p. 32). In this past decade, nearly half of GED® test takers were under 21 years of age (Zhang, Han, & Patterson, 2009). We know from talking to adult educators and can infer from demographic data on high school completion (Schott Foundation for Public Education, 2012) that many of these adolescents and young adults are men of color.

The GED® is sometimes considered a lesser alternative to or second chance for high school, and in some instances it is. However, for some young men who had few alternatives but to attend violent, chaotic, and toxic high schools, the GED® may be a good choice. The purpose of this chapter is to do what Tuck (2012) calls "reclaim the GED®" and to position GED® (which for purposes of this chapter will encompass HiSET® and TASC®) programs not as an alternative to high school, but as a counter-space in response and opposition to young men's previous school experiences. This chapter is based on an ethnography of one community-based urban GED® program and looks at the elements that make a GED® program a potential counter-space.

Counter-Space Defined

The concept of counter-space derives from critical race theory (CRT), which originated in legal studies (Delgado & Stefancic, 2012), but is now utilized across academic disciplines. CRT postulates that race is prevalent in any discussion of education and cannot be separated from a larger social context. The issue of race is full of contradiction and complexity, particularly as it is institutionalized. CRT further holds that the disparity in educational opportunity is an issue of civil rights and social justice (Closson, 2010; Heaney, 2000; Ladson-Billings, 2005).

Using this CRT framework, Solorzano and colleagues defined counter-space as a regenerating space that Black students created in White universities to escape discrimination. Counter-spaces are often created in same-race settings to acknowledge a marginalized group's life experiences (Solorzano, Ceja, & Yosso, 2000). They may be actual physical places of meeting or emotional spaces of voice, resistance, and healing. Carter (2007) calls these spaces "identity affirming counter-spaces" (p. 542).

Case and Hunter (2012) expand the definition of counter-space to include settings that promote emotional and psychological health for individuals who have experienced marginalization and oppression. Counter-spaces challenge deficit perspectives, creating interior and external spaces of resistance (hooks, 1989) that are characterized by counterstorytelling and solidarity.

This chapter expands the concept of counter-space to include GED® programs. These programs can serve as a space in response and opposition to young men's previous school experiences. Both CRT as the prevailing paradigm and counter-space as an operational concept are relevant because the participants are African American and Hispanic attending schools of color but within the United States where racial marginalizing is institutionalized and the prevailing cultural pedagogy is "White" (Grant, 1992, p. 112).

The Ethnographic Study: The Young Men and Prior Schooling

Javier, Dustin, Jamal, David, Shawn, and 11 other African American and Hispanic males of ages 16–25 were GED® students and participants in an ethnography of an ABE program in a large urban northeastern city. Note that all names and all names that accompany quotations are pseudonyms throughout this chapter. The program served 700 students annually in GED®, English for Speakers of Other Languages (ESOL), and literacy classes. The remainder of this chapter is based on the findings of this research (Schwartz, 2011, 2014).

The young men reported that their previous schools were unsafe or unjust spaces marked by frequent violence, abuse, excessive rules, drab surroundings, and what students perceived to be ethics violations. At best, their schools were nondescript and unpleasant spaces where neither teachers nor students wanted to be. These previous settings were not predominantly White schools, but racially diverse or predominantly Black schools with a racially diverse staff. The atmosphere was chaotic and tense, with frequent gang activity and bullying. Gun-related violence permeated many of the high schools, and the young men reported feeling unsafe both physically and emotionally. Abuse ranged from mild teasing and bullying to physical violation, from neglect to psychological mistreatment. Learners reported that inappropriate special education placement, racial profiling, and low expectations resulted in boredom. The young men stated that such an environment was normal to them.

The GED® Program as Counter-Space

In contrast to the toxic schools that the young men had left, the GED® program was a space of physical safety, voice, silence, emotional healing, and relationship. The young men viewed the GED® as a counter-space embodied in physical, ideological, and experiential dimensions (see Figure 4.1).

Physical Place and the Circle. The physical layout of a classroom elicited powerful feelings the moment students walked in. For Javier, Dustin,

Figure 4.1. Dimensions of GED® Counter-Space

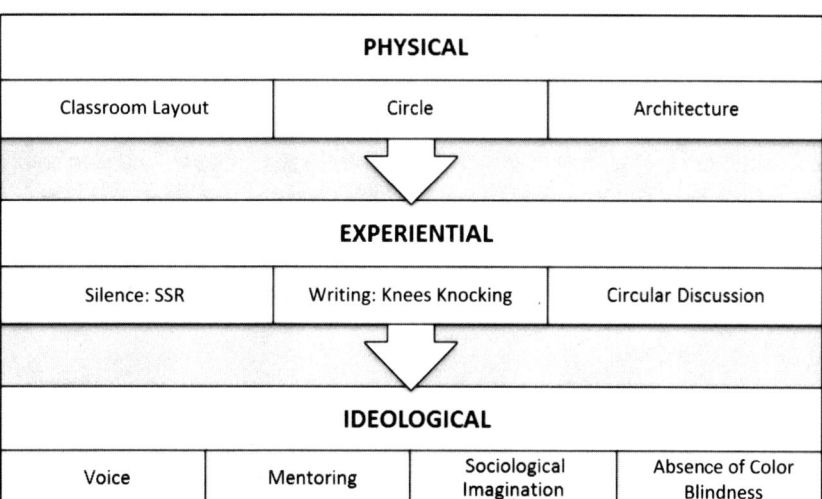

Jamal, David, and Shawn, the space did not "communicate" public school. They reported feeling safer because the physical configuration of furniture and dimensions of the room were in contrast to public schools with isolated classrooms, drab walls, police security, and barred windows. The GED® program was housed in two gymnasium-sized rooms with high ceilings and no walls between study groups. Learners perceived these open classrooms as spaces safe from the threat of violence. The rooms felt unconfined and not cramped. Javier said that the space allowed him to see what was going on. Dustin scoped the room before taking a seat; scanning brought a feeling of safety because he could "eye" the three wide doors for easy egress.

Within these large rooms, 8 to 12 small groups met around their own table. There was no physical separation between tables. Each circle was self-contained and intimate. There could be as many as 12 circles with 12 different activities. Participants spoke about the comfort of "my group" or "my space" in contrast to traditional classrooms of 30 students in rows and desks. Similar learning circles have deep roots in this country, reaching from Native American culture to adult education practice best exemplified at Highlander Folk School, where the open circle and rocking chair configuration are historic (Horton, 1998, p. 150).

The relationship between race and classroom architecture was not explicitly explored in this ethnography, but the significance of the physical setting and the learning circle was prevalent in the findings, especially as the space counters and looks different from past learning spaces.

Space for Voice. What does it mean to make room for voice within a program? Black feminists were among the first to articulate "coming to voice" and to use voice as resistance to oppression and marginalization. hooks (1989) describes this speaking up, speaking out, and telling your story, whether it be through writing, dissenting, discussion, public speaking, rap, or poetry. She wrote: "oppressed groups who have contained so many feelings—despair, rage, anguish—who do not speak for fear they won't be heard [for them] coming to voice is an act of resistance" (p. 12). This need to speak about the different dimensions of one's life begins the "process of education for critical consciousness" (p. 13).

In the same vein, the GED® program fostered spaces where the men could use this liberatory voice: in student councils, speaker forums, and discussion circles as well as in writing and in writing-sharing groups. These are democratic forums for dialogue and dissension, listening and speaking. Again, these spaces are not new to adult education, but speak to the very history of the field. Past examples are best epitomized by Danish folk schools, the Antigonish Movement, and Highlander (Jorgensen & Schwartz, 2012).

Among the most valued experiences of space for the men was writing. This was dedicated writing time within each small group; the goals of these 20-minute intensive sessions were to write for GED® practice and for their own "coming to voice" for healing. Writing created space to say what might not be spoken, and the men were often very candid and frequently wrote their pain.

The young men began by writing personal narratives about past educational experiences and trauma, often using journaling, poetry, and sometimes rap.

Writing seems a less risky initial approach to sharing pain—an opportunity to get the pain on paper, to examine, share, and sometimes ease it. Learners' journals frequently mentioned hardship, feelings of invisibility, and how "it feels in the heart of a man." The men wrote about their "pops being always locked up" and "moms never being around" and the impact that such events had on their progress in school. They wrote about daily racial microaggressions (Sue, 2010) that they experienced as Black males in a racialized society.

After writing, learning circles frequently engaged in what the program called "knees knocking": another space where students and tutors read the writing. Knees knocking was voluntary. Writers sat in a circle of chairs with no physical barrier between them, aiding listening and intimacy. The space is guarded, meaning that once the group starts no one new can enter. Total respect for the reader was expected, and responding to the content of the writing was primary, as shown in the following field note:

> Six young men sit in a circle of chairs with their knees almost touching. Justice reads his personal narrative. The other five listen, bending into the center trying to catch every word. The piece is about the writer's betrayal and brutal gang initiation. Fortunately, the beating was intercepted, and the writer got away with minor bruises. Yet the emotional trauma was evident. Once the writer finished reading, someone whispered, "That's OK, man, it happens to the best of us." The others nodded in agreement.

The goal of knees knocking was to understand the writer's experience, to acknowledge and affirm his voice, and to assist the writer in moving forward through his pain, as well as to grow as a writer. These spaces are not explicitly therapy; however, they do seem palliative.

In addition to sharing their writing, the learning circles discussed newspaper articles and history readings from the GED® book and other sources, attempting to make connections between the present and history—a space of intergenerational knowledge and voice. Mills (2000) calls this space "the sociological imagination" where an individual's problems are understood in relation to larger social and economic contexts (p. 5).

After reading about for-profit prisons, one circle discussed the connection between past physical slavery and current mental slavery precipitated by re-segregation of public education. Outside of school, stop and frisk policies and the mass incarceration of Black men continue to oppress. The group viewed this as a whole system set up for failure. While accepting responsibility for their own contributing behaviors, group members were invigorated when reflecting on the possibility that their own school failure may have been part of these larger systemic failures and institutionalized racism.

Research participants spoke about microaggressions on the job, in public places, and in the church. They agreed that discussions of race were crucial because there are few spaces to talk honestly about the "hard issues," and race is a hard issue "that everyone tries to avoid." Although the topic of race is often uncomfortable and complex, if it is not addressed, "another negative message is sent to these young men that this is another place where racism is avoided," stated Shawn. Shawn then went on to straightforwardly voice, "Yes, you are Black and you are starting the race from somewhere in the back" because race was never completely uprooted or addressed.

Space for Silence. Coming from crowded urban neighborhoods and chaotic schools, the men expressed appreciation for spaces to be quiet, to think, and to feel. In the GED® program, favorite spaces were the intentional silence during reading and writing that provided solitude with others. Thirty minutes of sustained silent reading (SSR) in each class was one such space. SSR is not unusual to K–12, but it may be less frequent in adult education. Typically, SSR is a designated period of silent reading when a whole class or school reads. The activity normally includes administrators, staff, teachers, and students, and in this GED® program, such was the case. Thirty minutes of each session were spent in SSR when often hundreds of learners in two large rooms were silently reading material of their choice. Fieldwork notes record the following dialogue and observation:

> "Take out your favorite book, sit back, relax and begin reading"—a voice from the microphone announces. David takes out a paperback with no cover; he reads with his tutor and his small group for 30 minutes—no moving, in complete silence.

This quiet space was counter to the constant chatter of many classrooms. Javier described SSR as "peace," giving him a sense of relaxation and focus. Knowing that to pass the GED® exam they needed to read often, participants reported SSR as a primary space that engaged them. Quiet was so rare in their lives—separated from cell phones, texting, the Internet, and television—this counter-space made room for self-reflection.

Silence is also healing. "A safe place" is free from physical and emotional harm or potential violence, but "a healing place" is where emotional residue rises to the surface where it can then be addressed. According to Rich (2009), we have underestimated the impact of all types of violence in and out of school and the "persistent psychological wounds" they cause to men in our inner cities (p. 12). Wounded individuals full of fear of failure and carrying unresolved pain cannot achieve a GED® until healing is addressed (Schwartz, Schwartz, & Osborne-Morris, 2012). The young men reported that they wanted to learn, but were often carrying so much pain underneath seemingly hard exteriors that concentration was impossible. The silent spaces of reading time proved palliative.

Both the silent reading and writing spaces provided think time. Neurological science has posited writing as a vehicle for thinking and a tool for cognitive restructuring (Menary, 2007). Thus, the combination of silence and writing provides potentially cognitive and therapeutic benefits. Silence is in a sense countercultural, and in that respect, it was a type of counter-space that was highly valued by the young men.

Mentoring Space. Mentoring is a recognized strategy for addressing the educational success of disengaged youth (Jekielek, Moore, Hair, & Scarupa, 2002; Miller, 2008). All five key informants reported that their mentors in the program were responsible for their reengagement. These relationships were emotionally intense, beginning at the GED® program, but sometimes extending outside into their personal lives. The men reported having strong positive feelings for their mentor (who could be a tutor, staff member, or a peer) and believed the relationship was instrumental in their development of self-esteem and mental health.

These affective relationships were a type of counter-space as places of openness and trust, as opposed to previous school experiences where trust was almost always absent. The term "affective relationship" is adapted from the term "affective talent" and emphasizes the connection between the affective and cognitive aspects in learning (Astin, 1984) as well as the spiritual domain (Palmer, 1998). This mentoring relationship is characterized by its holistic, reciprocal nature as well as by the absence of color/race blindness (Bonilla-Silva, 2003).

Holistic. These relationships are holistic in that they address the totality of the person. For example, Shawn and his tutor studied math and science (cognitive) but also discussed the pain of being placed in special education and fears of failure (emotional). Because the program was housed in a church, they both felt comfortable praying together about both the GED® and Shawn's fears (spiritual).

Emotional attachment is at the core of this mentoring relationship. The young men reported feeling and discussing a whole range of emotions while engaged in cognitive work. This is not surprising, as neurological research has determined that the brain does not separate emotions from cognition (Caine & Caine, 1994).

Javier described his relationship with Ms. Y, an internship coordinator, as one where he not only learned filing, computer, and appropriate workplace communication but also learned to "release stress and pressure and absorb the love" from her. The data were permeated with affective language; the men were not afraid to use phrases like "I got mad love for [my tutor]," "that's what I call love," and "he's on my back but that's because he cares."

It seems that the formation of affective relationships was in part a result of the mentors' affective talent (Astin, 1984) for empathetic communication. A mentor's expectation that the young men take personal responsibility for their learning is balanced by sensitivity to the social context that has played a critical role in inhibiting progress in the first place.

In addition to the emotional and cognitive dimensions, there was often a spiritual dimension to the mentoring relationship not uncommon in adult learning (Tisdell, 2008). As part of a faith-based initiative, the program was connected to a church; this connection made spiritual relationships not only commonplace but acceptable. For purposes of this discussion, spiritual relationships are defined as relationships that focus on the development of a religious faith, a spiritual inner life, and a relationship with God. Because prayer, Bible study, and worship through the church were voluntarily available, and the mentors were often members of the church, they frequently became spiritual guides and supports for the young men. This aspect of the affective relationship was culturally familiar to the young men, with the exception of David, who were all raised in the church and were open to and very accepting of spiritual support.

Reciprocal. In addition to being holistic, the relationships were reciprocal. These are adult-to-adult partnerships, sometimes of the same race and gender but also of mixed race and gender. Communication was characterized by dialogue, choice, autonomy, learner-centeredness, mutual respect, and equalitarianism—characteristics that define adult relationships (Knowles, 1970). Both participants in the relationship appeared to "share power." Often it was difficult to differentiate between tutors and students; all were together, sharing books they were reading, conversing and debating on current events, and negotiating the goals for the session.

Students provided emotional support to tutors as well. Dustin's mentor had a death in his family, and Dustin organized the sending of cards and gifts. Other men exchanged phone calls and text messages when a mentor was sick. They prayed for each other. David helped his tutor move to a new apartment.

Sometimes these relationships extended long beyond the program and included multiple mentoring roles: parent, older sibling, teacher, guidance counselor, career or college consultant, therapist, friend, colearner, spiritual advisor, and coworker.

Tutors helped with college tuition, rent, carfare, food, and clothes. They talked about getting sufficient sleep, the importance of completing homework, avoiding potentially harmful sexual activity, how to respond when approached by the police, and choosing the right friends. Shawn's mentor addressed Shawn's drug use and entrance to college. The tutor contacted drug programs, made follow-up phone calls to reengage Shawn, and finally paid his college entrance fee.

Sometimes the mentor advised about colleges and the admission process, college fairs, and financial aid. Mentors and learners attended college open houses. Intense emotional health issues were also sometimes broached—issues of loss, gangs, bullying, and reentry from prison. Mentors appeared to keep good boundaries, and connected to professional therapists and guidance counselors when appropriate.

Absence of Color/Race Blindness. Although the research participants were Black and Hispanic males and the majority of the tutors Black and Hispanic as well, the data were clear that the gender or race of the mentor in an affective relationship was not a salient concern to the young men. Gender and race were much less important than their mentor's expressions of care (Ladson-Billings, 1997).

However, what did seem to matter, and what speaks to counter-space, is that the mentor did not engage in color-blind or race-blind discourse. Color or race blindness is the paradigm held by many Whites, and some Blacks, that race and racism are no longer issues in America and that they no longer have the power they once held. It is also the negation of White privilege (Bonilla-Silva, 2003; Doob, 2013).

Whether White or Black, the mentor's capacity to address race and to open spaces for dialogue around race's impact on learning and equality of opportunity was necessary for counter-space development. The ability to avoid color-blind discourse that allows for easy negation of racism and neither challenges nor examines current racism seemed to be more crucial in a mentor than gender or race.

GED® tutors with this color-blind schema appear to have difficulty creating counter-spaces that are emotionally safe for dialogue that engages issues around racial micro- and macroaggressions that impact Black men in America and their educational pursuit. Counter-spaces do not deny individual responsibility or excuse lack of effort and lackadaisical intellectual engagement, but the concept does recognize the systemic forces of marginalization and oppression that still exist. Therefore, effective counter-spaces must have mentors who recognize and can verbalize the impact that racism continues to have on African American and other young men of color.

Conclusion

In view of these findings, what recommendations can be made for GED® programs as they engage African American males and young men of color? First, be intentional about creating counter-spaces and strategically plan with young men. Elicit their ideas and partner with them in designing or rethinking learning spaces. Don't underestimate the impact that past schooling experiences—violence before, after, and during school—has had on the young men. Think about ways to make learning spaces emotionally as well as physically safe. Encourage young men to talk and write about prior school experiences and their hopes for a different experience in your adult education program.

Second, do not underestimate the power of physical space. Within the financial and spatial limitations you have, think "outside the box" about how your physical space can be counter-space to previous schools. Simply rearrange the tables, desks, or chairs to create small groups within a classroom—the less the space looks like school the better. Third, create experiential spaces like SSR and knees knocking as well as discussion circles that make room for small-group learning and embrace both voice and silence.

Fourth, with your staff and volunteers encourage critical reflexivity that examines schemas toward race and racism and examines how these schemas help or hinder the establishment of counter-spaces that are holistic, reciprocal, and are absent of color/race blindness. Engage your staff and volunteers in the hard conversations—communication around race. Especially if your group is predominantly White, it will be necessary to explore White privilege and how it manifests in relationships with men of color. It will be important to explore biases, stereotypes, and color-blind thinking with the ultimate goal of transformative learning for all. Finally, actively work toward creating counter-space through physical, ideological, and experiential dimensions with the goal of engaging previously marginalized GED® populations.

References

Astin, A. W. (1984). Student involvement: A developmental theory for higher education. *Journal of College Student Personnel, 25*, 297–308.
Bonilla-Silva, E. (2003). *Racism without racists: Color-blind racism and the persistence of racial inequality in the United States.* Lanham, MD: Rowman & Littlefield.
Caine, R., & Caine, G. (1994). *Making connections: Teaching and the human brain.* Menlo Park, CA: Innovative Learning Publications.
Carter, D. J. (2007). Why the Black kids sit together at the stairs: The role of identity-affirming counter-space in a predominantly White high school. *The Journal of Negro Education, 76*(4), 542–555.
Case, A., & Hunter, C. (2012). Counter-spaces: A unit of analysis for understanding the role of settings in marginalized individuals' adaptive responses to oppression. *American Journal of Community Psychology, 50*(1–2), 257–270.
Closson, R. (2010). Critical race theory and adult education. *Adult Education Quarterly, 60*(3), 261–283.
College Board Advocacy & Policy Center. (2013). *The educational experience of young men of color.* New York, NY. Retrieved from http://youngmenofcolor.collegeboard.org
Delgado, R., & Stefancic, J. (2012). *Critical race theory: An introduction* (2nd ed.). New York: NYU Publications.
Doob, C. (2013). *Social inequality and social stratification in US society.* Upper Saddle River, NJ: Pearson.
Grant, C. (1992). *Research in multicultural education: From the margins to the mainstream.* London, UK: Falmer Press.
Heaney, T. (2000). Adult education and society. In A. L. Wilson & E. R. Hayes (Eds.), *Handbook of adult and continuing education* (pp. 559–572). San Francisco, CA: Jossey-Bass.
hooks, b. (1989). *Talking back: Thinking feminist, thinking Black.* Cambridge, MA: South End Press.
Horton, M. (1998). *The long haul.* New York, NY: Teachers College Press.
Jekielek, S., Moore, K., Hair, E., & Scarupa, H. (2002). *Mentoring: A promising strategy for youth development.* Washington, DC: Child Trends Research Brief.
Jorgensen, S., & Schwartz, J. (2012). Continuing the legacy: Democracy and education practice. *Journal of Research and Practice for Adult Literacy, Secondary and Basic Education, 1*(3), 179–184.
Knowles, M. S. (1970). *The modern practice of adult education.* Englewood Cliffs, NJ: Cambridge Adult Education.
Ladson-Billings, G. (1997). *Dreamkeepers: Successful teachers of African-American children.* Hoboken, NJ: Wiley.
Ladson-Billings, G. (2005). The evolving role of critical race theory in educational scholarship. *Race Ethnicity and Education, 8*(1), 115–119.

Menary, R. (2007). Writing as thinking. *Language Sciences, 29,* 621–632.
Miller, D. (2008). *Man up: Recruiting and retaining African-American male mentors: Executive summary.* Baltimore, MD: National Urban League.
Mills, C. W. (2000). *The sociological imagination* (40th ed.). New York, NY: Oxford University Press.
Palmer, P. (1998). *The courage to teach.* San Francisco, CA: Jossey-Bass.
Rachal, J., & Bingham, M. (2004). The adolescentizing of the GED®. *Adult Basic Education: An Interdisciplinary Journal for Adult Literacy Educational Planning, 14*(1), 32–44.
Rich, J. (2009). *Wrong place, wrong time.* Baltimore, MD: John Hopkins University Press.
Schott Foundation for Public Education. (2012). *The urgency of now: The Schott 50 state report on public education and Black males.* Retrieved from http://www.schottfoundation.org/urgency-of-now.pdf
Schwartz, J. (2011). *Engaging out of school males in learning* (Doctoral dissertation). Ann Arbor, MI: ProQuest.
Schwartz, J. (2014). Classrooms of spatial justice: Counter-spaces and young men of color in a GED® program. *Adult Education Quarterly, 64*(2), 110–127.
Schwartz, J., Schwartz, P. (Producers), & Osborne-Morris, R. (Documentarian). (2012). *A new normal: Young men of color, trauma, and engagement in learning* [Documentary]. Retrieved from https://lagcc-cuny.digication.com/joni_schwartz_d_ed/Documentary
Solorzano, D., Ceja, M., & Yosso, T. (2000). Critical race theory, racial microaggressions, and campus racial climate: The experiences of African-American college students. *The Journal of Negro Education, 69*(1/2), 60–73.
Sue, D. W. (2010). *Microaggressions in everyday life.* Hoboken, NJ: Wiley.
Tisdell, E. (2008). Spirituality and adult learning. In S. B. Merriam (Ed.), *New Directions for Adult and Continuing Education: No. 119. Third update on adult learning theory* (pp. 27–36). San Francisco, CA: Jossey-Bass.
Tuck, E. (2012). *Urban youth and school pushout: Gateways, get-aways, and the GED.* New York, NY: Routledge.
Tuck, E., & Neofotistos, I. (Eds.). (2013). *Youth to youth guide to the GED®.* Retrieved from http://sites.newpaltz.edu/youthguideged/wp-content/uploads/sites/9/2013/04/Youth-to-Youth-Guide-to-the-GED-Final.pdf
Yosso, T., Ceja, M., Smith, W., & Solorzano, D. (2009). Critical race theory, racial microaggressions, and campus racial climate for Latina/o undergraduates. *Harvard Educational Review, 79,* 659–690.
Zhang, J., Han, M. Y., & Patterson, M. (2009). *Young GED® examinees and their performance on the GED® tests.* Washington, DC: American Council on Education.

JONI SCHWARTZ is an associate professor in the Humanities Department at LaGuardia Community College, City University of New York.

5 | *This chapter will center on the continuing impact of systemic and persistent educational trauma experienced by Black and Latino males and how trauma affects their current learning. The young men's counterstories from a phenomenological study and documentary are included.*

A New Normal: Young Men of Color, Trauma, and Engagement in Learning

Carlyle Van Thompson, Paul J. Schwartz

Black males killing Black males, White males killing Black males, and White police officers killing Black males: these are the tragic circumstances that we face in this so-called postracial society where we have twice elected a Black male President. Barack Hussein Obama, his charismatic wife Michelle, and their two daughters have changed the iconography of Blackness in profound ways. Despite this positive imagery, almost every day across America we are confronted with tragic news concerning the shootings and deaths of young Black males. The prevalence of racial violence vibrantly underscores the institutionalization of White male supremacist culture.

Regardless of skin color or class, young Black males are too often viewed as inherently aggressive, dangerous, and criminal. There is little evidence that change will come any time soon. The snarling winds of White supremacist culture create a perpetual winter in the lives of many Black people, leaving Black communities in a nihilistic state of hopelessness. As in the past, when wealthy White male landowners exploited free Black labor, Black males still represent a disposable commodity and a pervasive threat to White America's notions of security.

The tragic shooting of Jonathan Ferrell, a former Florida A&M football player who recently moved to the Charlotte, NC area, provides dramatic evidence of White America's notion of safety and security. After he had a horrible car crash, the 24-year-old escaped through the back window and walked, injured, to knock on the nearest door for help. Soon, Ferrell would be dead. The White neighbor he asked for assistance called 911, reporting Ferrell was attempting to break down her door (McLaughlin, 2014). One of the responding White male police officers shot the unarmed Ferrell 10 times. We wonder what explanation the police department will give to Ferrell's fiancée, his family, and his community. This chapter aims to help educators understand the profound impact of trauma on our young men. It will identify approaches that will help educators aid learners in confronting effects of past trauma.

Theoretical Framework

Two texts supply a framework for our discussion. Judith Herman's (1992) *Trauma and Recovery* describes the stages of trauma recovery. Herman divides the process of healing from trauma into three stages: establishing a safe environment, remembrance and mourning, and reconnection. The task of Herman's first stage, establishing a safe environment, involves naming the problem, restoring control, and establishing a safe environment (Herman, 1992). The task of the second stage, remembrance and mourning, involves retelling the trauma story and reconstructing the traumatic memory so that it can be "integrated into the survivor's life story" (p. 175). Reconnection, the final stage, involves the task of creating a future. Complementing Herman's stages of trauma recovery, selections from Frederick Douglass's (1845) autobiography, *Narrative of the Life of Frederick Douglass, an American Slave*, provide a historical context.

The chapter remains true to the tenets of critical race theory that emphasize the importance of the voices of people of color (Delgado & Stephanic, 2001) and the centrality of experiential knowledge through counterstorytelling (Solorzano, 1998). It will present the findings from a phenomenological study that posed the research question, "How does trauma experienced by young men of color affect their learning engagement and their access of counseling and support services?"

Readers will hear directly from our research participants, 20 young men, ages 18–27. The following data collection techniques were employed for the ethnographic study: a questionnaire soliciting the young men's experiences with trauma, in-depth semistructured interviews with open-ended questioning, and focus groups and member-checking activities where participants came together and gave feedback. The names used in the study are pseudonyms.

Findings

The findings indicate that many young Black and Latino men are coming to the educational setting with posttraumatic stress (PTS) that they perceive as a normal part of life. Data suggest that for the young men, trauma is an ongoing, sometimes daily, series of experiences. We use the term "new normal" to describe the cumulative traumatic experiences, in and out of school, that the young men described as normal in their lives. All the participants resonated with the concept of *trauma*, understood trauma as "a given" in their lives, and accepted the inevitability of it. The shared wounds caused by past trauma for many young Black and Latino men may be better understood in a larger historical context and framework that further complicates both the injury and the healing necessary for optimal engagement in learning.

Establishing a Safe Environment. The problem of establishing a safe environment has been critical for Black males in American society from the chaotic times of enslavement to the present. As Herman (1992) states,

> Trauma robs the victim of a sense of power and control; the guiding principle of recovery is to restore power and control to the survivor. The first task of recovery is to establish the survivor's safety. This task takes precedence over all others, for no other therapeutic work can possibly succeed if safety has not been adequately secured. (p. 159)

Whether enslaved or free, Black males lived in a society where violence was always present and unpredictable. Laws during the period of enslavement and the Jim Crow laws and Black Codes that came afterward were designed for the enduring socioeconomic disenfranchisement of Black people.

Frederick Douglass is one of the most important Black voices with regard to the issues of Black male subjectivity and democracy within the paradoxical context of America's White supremacist culture. In terms of safety, Douglass's (1845) narrative provides examples where Black male slaves were maimed or killed. Today, reports of young Black males being killed in cities like Chicago and New York create ongoing trauma for young Black males and their families. The pervasiveness of trauma among the young men in the study and documentary was evident as they spoke about horrific experiences as if they were talking about eating dinner or going to the store. Their words and conversational tone connoted resignation that this is how their life is: Nigel said, "Losing people—the reason why it's normal to me is that it happens a lot." Donovan said, "A guy I grew up with, he got shot, whatever...it was the second death in a year...I lost my best friend, and my cousin was killed." The young men related to each others' life histories that included gang violence, threats with weapons, and violent deaths.

Teachers and staff in educational settings, however, might not understand trauma as a habitual, inevitable, expected part of life for learners. Noguera (2003) captures the disparity in school experiences that often exists between students and their teachers. When discussing the climate of violence that is typical in an economically depressed inner-city middle school where he was working, he stated, "I became increasingly aware of the fact that many adults at this school had no idea of how kids experience violence in their everyday lives" (p. 112).

The fear of constantly witnessing and experiencing violence is no doubt a major reason why students disengage from learning and drop out of school (Schwartz & Schwartz, 2012). Although the participants are overcomers—each one either graduated high school or obtained his General Equivalency Diploma (GED®)—the impact of traumatic experiences on their emotional health and sense of safety and stability was evident.

Now, as in the past, legal dictates in America are often designed to provide socioeconomic benefit to the dominant White male society. Paradoxically, legal issues such as racial profiling have created another slave-like reality manifest in the prison–industrial complex (Coyle, Campbell, & Neufeld, 2003), where Black males (many in the prime of their lives) are facing life in prison for drug-related criminal activity. There is a clear connection between Black bodies and White wealth and leisure, just as when Douglass lived.

Detention centers and prisons full of Black and Latino males provide tremendous economic benefit to rural White communities in terms of jobs and services; this cheap and slave-like labor force is also beneficial to major corporations that use prisoners for numerous tasks. The Corrections Corporation of America (CCA), the nation's largest owner of private prisons, has seen its revenue climb by more than 500% in the past two decades (Kroll, 2013). And CCA wants to get much, much bigger: Last year, the company made an offer to 48 governors to buy and operate their state-funded prisons. But what made CCA's pitch to those governors shocking was that it included an occupancy requirement, a clause demanding that the state keep those newly privatized prisons at least 90% full at all times, regardless of whether crime was rising or falling. With a deal like this in place, state and city law enforcement policies would be designed to support the incarceration of the most vulnerable populations. Not surprisingly, private prison companies such as CCA and the Management and Training Corporation have supported and helped write "three-strike" and "truth-in-sentencing" laws that drive up prison populations (p. 4). Between 1954 and 2004, incarceration of African Americans increased by 829% (98,000 to 910,000; Mauer, 2006). One New York study showed that minorities were more likely than Whites to receive jail time for misdemeanors and property crimes resulting in an additional 4000 sentences a year. The impact of penal policy on our young men can be seen in the educational system.

Educational Trauma. For the purposes of this chapter, educational trauma is defined as a trauma that, according to participants, was experienced in middle school or high school, before and after school sessions, with the perpetrators being peers or teachers. Experiences of trauma included, but were not limited to, verbal abuse in the form of ongoing name calling, bullying, condescending and demeaning language by teachers and school officials, out of control classrooms, and criminalization of school settings.

Educational abuse was noted in statements made to participants by their teachers that revealed low expectations of student's ability and potential. These messages were seared into the young men's consciousness. Terrance stated: "Teachers said to us, 'I don't care if you don't learn, I still get paid.' Teachers don't care. No motivation. Teachers basically told us the answers . . . made me feel stupid, a little lower." Feelings of inferiority, incompetence, and even hopelessness can become internalized when perpetuated by supposed educators making demeaning remarks.

Study participants reported these events with clarity and detail, almost as if they had happened yesterday. The impact of early school experiences had traveled with the young men to other learning environments and was manifested in trauma responses. The young men were less trustful, less assertive, and wary of educational settings. They described how they often "scoped" classrooms as they entered to make sure they were safe. They chose to sit in the back of the room to make sure that everything was okay before they engaged with the teacher and other students. "When you come into a new environment, you don't feel safe at all. You know if you don't say the right thing it's gonna stick with you throughout the semester, year, whatever," Rudy explained. He recalled being teased and taunted with demeaning racist "jokes" by White classmates in elementary school. Lowering his head, he reflected, "Some were funny, but they stick. . . ." (gesturing with his fist toward his heart as if the cutting remarks had settled deep within his being).

The need to establish safe classrooms is foundational. During the interviews, focus groups, and member-checking activities, participants claimed ownership, stating that they felt part of the process. A therapeutic climate was created. This was not therapy, but the provision of "safe spaces" where healing could occur. These were spaces where the young men felt empowered, emotionally safe, and grateful to be given a voice and to have their voices heard and valued. Sharing in a safe environment with mutual support led to a normalizing of their experiences. This helped participants to understand and name past experiences as trauma, thus helping restore control. The creation of a safe space that gives voice to marginalized experiences aligns with emancipatory transformative learning that espouses inclusion, empowerment, self-expression, and critical thinking (Johnson-Bailey & Alfred, 2006).

Remembrance and Mourning. After the educator or helper has established a safe environment and a personal relationship with the young male student, as a trauma survivor the student needs a new language to rename experiences that have been nameless and voiceless. According to Herman (1992), "Remembering and telling the truth about terrible events are prerequisites both for the restoration of the social order and for the healing of individual victims" (p. 1).

In *Narrative of the Life of Frederick Douglass, an American Slave*, Douglass (1845) also allows us to connect to the issues of remembrance and mourning. It is important to remember that Douglass was a free man when he wrote his narrative, and the memories of his horrific days flooded into his mind. At one point, Douglass commented that the pen that he was writing with could be placed in the gash in his foot. Here we have that symbiotic relationship between writing and the body that has endured years of horrific violence and neglect. Despite years of trauma, Douglass was able to write and speak himself into existence. He published three autobiographies and became a national spokesman against the enslavement of Black people. Young Black and Latino males who have experienced trauma also have the ability to write and speak themselves into existence, if they have the proper guidance and encouragement.

According to Herman (1992), the ultimate goal in trauma recovery is to put the trauma story into words. The study and documentary participants were provided emotionally safe spaces and given an opportunity to tell their counterstories. The young men were allowed to "come to voice" and to overcome what Ken Hardy (2011) called "learned voicelessness." Hardy asserted that it is a task of the subjugated to advocate for themselves, to challenge the belief that it is not worth speaking up, to unlearn the behavior from being taught to be silent, and not to "speak unless spoken to."

The study revealed that writing about traumatic experiences as a way to get the pain on the paper can be an effective tool for recovery from trauma. Several participants came to the study by writing about their pain through personal narratives in the classroom setting. The following excerpts from the young men's writing suggest the power of these counterstories and their healing potential:

- "I'm getting healing through writing, because I'm venting it out...I'm feeling better."—Michael
- "My story was like a rock in my heart that I had to break down and let all my feelings out on paper."—Stephan
- "If I didn't tell this story it [the trauma] would drag on in me and never let me go. I felt I had to tell this story so people may do the same thing I did. They will know how to overcome the situation."—Kami

Data analysis from the study suggests that the writing of personal narratives for young men of color is a good way of broaching issues of trauma in the classroom and in the counseling setting. In "Engaging Out of School Males in Learning," an educational ethnography, Schwartz (2010) explored the therapeutic nature of writing for young men of color in greater detail.

It is critically important that these young males see themselves in classroom texts and other materials that are used in the classroom. As Douglass did, these young Black men can remember and mourn the tragedies and disappointments in their lives and move on. Richard Wright and Chester Bomar Himes are 20th-century Black male writers who had difficult childhoods, but were able to write themselves into existence through both nonfiction and fiction.

It is also important for educators to understand the various ways young men cope with or *come to voice* about their trauma and to whom they disclose their experiences. Of the 20 study participants, 16 had not sought out nor participated in formal counseling. They did not believe that counseling "would do any good," and they felt that they just "have to bear it," or "tough it out" for themselves—the "it" being traumatic experiences. Damien explained his mistrust of counseling: "We grew up self-healing. We can handle it." Jason concurred: "I have to handle this myself. I can stand up—not be a punk."

However, the four young men who had participated in counseling thought it was helpful. Stephan, who went to counseling due to family loss and past school trauma, said issues of trust were crucial, "Statistically, counseling works...but, it's finding someone you trust."

Kami stated that before counseling he had not known how to process traumatic events in his school, neighborhood, and home. Both Stephan and Kami were apprehensive about counseling. Kami described his feelings going into counseling: "I had intense fear, anxiety, angry. I felt out of control....I thought I was going crazy. I had lack of power and control but I saw that connection [counseling]."

Kami, whose young niece had been shot and killed during a children's birthday party and who had also lost his father, became very emotional when recalling these experiences during the interview. He engaged in counseling and spoke positively about its benefits.

Herman (1992) warned that telling the trauma story inevitably "plunges the survivor into profound grief." She wrote, "Reclaiming the ability to feel the range of emotions, including grief, must be understood as an act of resistance.... The survivor frequently resists mourning, not only out of fear but also out of pride" (p. 188). Herman's strategic approach to resistance seems especially fitting for young men, helping them to reframe mourning as "an act of courage rather than humiliation" (p. 202).

Reconnection. In the final stage of trauma recovery, reconnection occurs with self, with others, and often with God or a spiritual, greater-than-self reality. According to Herman (1992), after having safely confronted the reality of trauma in one's life and "mourned the old self that trauma destroyed," survivors must develop a new self, with new relationships, new beliefs, and new meaning since "helplessness and isolation are at the core experiences of psychological trauma" (Herman, 1992, pp. 196–197). Participants in the project were discovering their new selves during the interviews, focus groups, and member-checking activities. Although this was not formal group therapy, a therapeutic climate was created that provided "spaces" where healing could occur. The young men reconnected with self, acknowledging and validating their experiences as integrated into their lives, helping them reconnect and become whole.

Participants experienced reconnection with others. They encouraged each other, not only verbally but also with their shared enthusiasm and willingness to work on the project. The intentional efforts from all who worked on the project conveyed hope, confidence, belief, and trust that counteracted the hurtful voices and contributed mightily to the participants' feeling empowered. Hearing each other's experiences and being able to name the formally wordlessness of trauma helped the young men to know that they were not alone. They gave voice to unspoken fears.

Originally, groups were scheduled for one hour, but groups ran well over the time because the young men did not want to stop. Many participants commented that they enjoyed the group very much, felt open and willing to share their traumatic experiences, and felt "relieved" and very good after the group. They also said that they were "grateful" to be a part of a group talking about their own lived experiences. Data suggest that these research groups were therapeutic to the young men because participants were all male, shared the same type of traumatic experiences, and felt that their experience as men of color was unique. They found that the group was confidential enough to allow them to share deep feelings. Many said that they felt free to talk about traumatic experiences, especially as they related to education, and trauma's impact on current engagement in learning.

The participants also saw a purpose outside of themselves. They wanted their voices to help other young men and educators. The reciprocal nature of the relationships between participants and interviewers made the difference. This type of reciprocity and interaction can occur when helpers (adult educators, counselors, mentors, and life coaches) genuinely and intentionally see and appreciate these young men and their experiences, believe in them, and draw out their strengths and abilities.

In the confrontation with the slave master Covey and in the final chapter of Douglass's (1845) narrative where Douglass relates his escape from slavery, we have the theme of reconnection. Covey is one of the most abusive slave masters to be found in the canon of slave narratives; he was always spying on his slaves and finding fault with them, whippings would often follow. Douglass relates his decisive fight: "This battle with Mr. Covey was the turning-point in my career as a slave. It rekindled the few expiring embers of freedom, and revived within me a sense of my own manhood. It recalled the departed self-confidence, and inspired me again with a determination to be free" (p. 104). As Douglass had his hands around Covey's throat, he experienced an epiphany of subjectivity: "My long-crushed spirit rose, cowardice departed, bold defiance took its place; and I now resolved that, however long I might remain a slave in fact, I did not hesitate to let it be known of me, that the White man who expected to succeed in whipping, must also succeed in killing me" (p. 105).

The transformation of Douglass is analogous to the metamorphic transformation that many Black and Latino males can experience in the classroom. Despite how the dominant White society repeatedly criminalizes Black males, the educational experience can empower them to change their lives and circumstances. Thus, the adult education setting can become a site of emancipatory transformative learning (Johnson-Bailey & Alfred, 2006) where young men of color can have positive experiences through honest dialogue, a caring environment, and an intentional minimizing of the power relationship between educator and learner. Michael Lapsley (2012) said that the goal for trauma survivors is to acknowledge the past, and the pain, but not to be its prisoner. In the final chapter, Douglass discussed the paradoxical nature of his escape: "The wretchedness of slavery, and the blessedness of freedom, were perpetually before me" (Douglass, 1845, p. 142). Too many young Black and Latino males who have been traumatized feel locked down and oppressed by the wretched conditions in which they live, but there are countless examples of men who have become free and blessed with possibilities that they could hardly imagine.

Implications for Practice

We were encouraged by the enthusiasm of the young men in the study. This enthusiasm translates into genuine engagement with learning and can be inspired by practitioners through integration of the following principles into pedagogy and therapeutic intervention. First, utilize texts and classroom materials that young men can relate to such as reading topics that include traumatic experiences and historical and present-day racial violence and injustices. In career preparation and training settings, the materials and discussions might include the work experiences of men of color whose racial identities have historically limited access to employment. Incorporating learner experiences not only promotes engagement but also provides resources for learning opportunities that enhance understanding and application. Second, encourage young men of color to voice their counterstories by writing. As research (Schwartz, 2010) has shown, this contemplative practice of expressing deeply significant experiences is a source of healing, and, especially for adult basic education learners, also a means of enhancing the technical skills of writing. In addition, because the experiences of men of color have been ignored or marginalized, their stories challenge commonly held beliefs of the larger society, and practitioners in particular, about how the world works. Third, promote learners' active participation in class discussions and support groups that will allow their voices to be heard and valued. Fourth, foster empowerment and create an environment of trust and safety through meaningful activities such as writing about and sharing experiences in small groups. As the participants in this study clearly convey, the creation of a safe space is critical to their engagement. This implies that practitioners may need to be intentional about helping young men of color to feel safe in their classrooms. Regardless of the educational context, the intersection of race, class, and gender influences learner experiences in the classroom, and for men of color connecting learning to lived experience is a necessary ingredient for engagement and transformation (Johnson-Bailey & Alfred, 2006; Sheared, 1999). The lessons learned and approaches presented here can benefit educators and counselors by increasing an understanding of and appreciation for their students and their students' experiences, which will often be very different from their own. If this society is truly to be a place of possibility, it is critical that young Black and Latino males have the agency associated with a truly democratic and postracial society.

References

Coyle, A., Campbell, A., & Neufeld, R. (Eds.). (2003). *Capitalist punishment: Prison privatization and human rights*. Atlanta, GA: Clarity Press.

Delgado, R., & Stephanic, J. (2001). *Critical race theory: An introduction.* New York: NY University Press.

Douglass, F. (1845). *Narrative of the life of Frederick Douglass, an American slave, written by himself.* Boston, MA: Anti-Slavery Office, Elegant Ebooks.

Hardy, K. (2011, December 11). Insights from Dr. Kenneth Hardy [Web log post]. Retrieved from http://traumatreatment.blogspot.com/2011/12/insights-from-dr-kenneth-hardy.html

Herman, J. (1992). *Trauma and recovery.* New York, NY: Basic Books.

Johnson-Bailey, J., & Alfred, M. (2006). Transformational teaching and the practices of Black women adult educators. In E. W. Taylor (Ed.), *New Directions for Adult and Continuing Education: No. 109. Fostering transformative learning in the classroom: Challenges and innovations* (pp. 49–58). San Francisco, CA: Jossey-Bass.

Kroll, A. (2013, September 19). This is how private prison companies make millions even when crime rates fall. *Mother Jones.* Retrieved from http://www.motherjones.com/mojo/2013/09/private-prisons-occupancy-quota-cca-crime

Lapsley, M. (2012). *Redeeming the past: My journey from freedom fighter to healer.* Maryknoll, NY: Orbis Books.

Mauer, M. (2006). *Race to incarcerate.* New York, NY: The New Press.

McLaughlin, E. (2014, January 28). 2nd grand jury indicts officer in shooting of ex-FAMU football player. *CNN U.S.* Retrieved from http://www.cnn.com/2014/01/27/us/north-carolina-police-shooting/

Noguera, P. (2003). *City schools and the American dream: Reclaiming the promise of public education.* New York, NY: Teachers College Press.

Schwartz, J. (2010). *Engaging out of school males in learning* (Doctoral dissertation). Retrieved from http://hdl.rutgers.edu/1782.2/rucore10001500001.ETD.000052893

Schwartz, P., & Schwartz, J. (Producers). (2012). *A new normal: Young men of color, trauma, and engagement in learning* [Videotape]. New York: City University of New York.

Sheared, V. (1999). Giving voice: Inclusion of African American students' polyrhythmic realities in adult basic education. In T. C. Guy (Ed.), *New Directions for Adult and Continuing Education: No. 82. Providing culturally relevant education: A challenge for the 21st century* (pp. 33–48). San Francisco, CA: Jossey-Bass.

Solorzano, D. (1998). Critical race theory, racial and gender microaggressions, and the experiences of Chicana and Chicano scholars. *International Journal of Qualitative Studies in Education, 11,* 121–136.

CARLYLE VAN THOMPSON *is a professor in the Department of English at Medgar Evers College, City University of New York.*

PAUL J. SCHWARTZ *is a faculty crisis counselor at New York City College of Technology, City University of New York.*

6

This chapter shares findings from a qualitative study on reentry adult Black males' postsecondary education experiences and identifies strategies to help this population matriculate through college and graduate.

The Reentry Adult College Student: An Exploration of the Black Male Experience

Dionne Rosser-Mims, Glenn A. Palmer, Pamela Harroff

Introduction

A rapidly changing global market demands a high-skilled labor force. The challenge for postsecondary education is to keep pace with demand and to meet the educational attainment needs of the 21st-century adult learner (Gast, 2013; Southern Region Education Board [SREB], 2010). Research indicates that approximately 60% of the fastest growing occupations require an associate's degree and 46% require a bachelor's degree or higher (Grummon, 2009). As a result of current economic conditions, record numbers of adult learners/nontraditional students are returning to postsecondary and vocational programs to retool and remain competitive in today's workplace.

Nationally, it is predicted that college enrollment for students of age 25 and older will continue to increase at a higher rate than enrollment of traditional-age students (Census Bureau of Labor Statistics, 2010; Gast, 2013; Grummon, 2009; Hauptman, 2008; SREB, 2010). This population of adult learners all too often enters or reenters the college environment lacking preparation for college-level work. They are also ill-prepared to balance family, work, and school. These conditions have made retaining these students problematic, particularly in distance-learning formats (Kazis et al., 2007; Levy, 2007; Park & Choi, 2009; Tyler-Smith, 2006).

Black males, the focus of this chapter, are disproportionately underrepresented in higher education relative to their total population numbers (Harper & Harris, 2012; Journal of Blacks in Higher Education [JBHE], 2013; Wood, 2011). According to the Schott Foundation for Public Education's (2012) *50 State Report on Public Education and Black Males*, only 52% of Black male ninth graders graduate from high school four years later, compared to 58% of Latino male ninth graders and 78% of White, non-Latino male ninth graders. Years later, Black males find themselves back in the college setting to pick up where they left off due to job loss, their status as returning military veterans, promotion aspirations, and dissatisfaction with status in life (Kasworm, 2002, 2003; Ross-Gordon, 2005; Ross-Gordon & Brown-Haywood, 2000).

The purpose of this chapter is to shed light on the experiences of reentry adult male college students, in particular Black males. We wanted to give voice to this marginalized group's lived experiences and to understand how those experiences shaped their paths to reentering college. This chapter also explores how colleges are supporting the adult reentry Black male student population in order to increase their retention and graduation rates. To address these topics, a qualitative study was conducted, guided by the following questions:

1. What are the major barriers to Black adult males' reentry to college?
2. What challenges do Black adult males experience during the reentry process?
3. What are Black adult males' major sources of support?

Theoretical Framework

Examining the experiences of reentry adult men of color, given the centrality of race, necessitates the use of a critical race theoretical (CRT) framework. From a CRT perspective, the lack of opportunity for quality education and schooling is not coincidental, but directly relates to the interplay of the socioeconomic forces that have thwarted Black Americans' efforts to escape poverty and its social ramifications (Howard, 2013; Ladson-Billings, 1998). Therefore, this discussion of Black men's experiences returning to college would be incomplete without focusing on the experience of Black Americans in the public school system. The low representation of Black males in college could be attributed in part to systemic barriers such as enrollment in poor school districts, high dropout rates in middle and high schools, high rates of incarceration, high rates of homicide, and chronic health problems (Duncan & Magnuson, 2005; Fryer & Levitt, 2006; Howard, 2013). The Black men who matriculate through college often struggle with the rigor of academic challenges if they were not properly prepared during the formative years of their schooling (Cuyjet, 1997, 2006; JBHE, 2013).

In the following section, we explore the educational trajectory for Black males in education that has resulted in the growing population of adult Black male reentry college students.

Educational Trajectory: Historical and Contemporary Patterns

In this study, Black men are defined as individuals who have traced their cultural or ethnic heritage to the Americas, the Caribbean, or Africa. Of the approximately 15 million students enrolled in higher education in the United States, less than 5% are Black males (Hauptman, 2008). According to Strayhorn (2008), the enrollment patterns of Blacks in higher education today mirror the enrollment patterns of the mid-1970s. Black males tend to enroll in two-year or technical schools and in historically Black colleges and universities (Harper & Griffin, 2011). They tend to have fewer financial resources than their White counterparts—to attend K–12 schools with fewer resources, lower per student expenditures, and less experienced teachers (Harper, 2012; Hucks, 2011).

While there are numerous studies that focus specifically on traditional and nontraditional Black women and their journey through the educational process (Coker, 2003; Johnson-Bailey, 2001; Sealey-Ruiz, 2007), very few empirical studies have focused on the foray of Black males as they try to navigate the challenges of returning to higher education as adult learners. Consequently, many institutions face low retention rates among this population. They do not understand the complex lived experiences of Black American male reentry college students and, therefore, are ill-equipped to meet their academic and social needs (Aslanian, 2001; Battle, Alderman-Swain, & Tyner, 2005; Cuyjet, 2006; Ross-Gordon, 2005).

Method

To gain a deeper understanding of the educational experiences of reentry adult Black male learners, an interpretive qualitative approach was used in this study (Denzin, 1989; Merriam, 1998; Strauss & Corbin, 1993). The sample population for this study comprised 15 Black males ranging in age from 25 to 45 who had previously attended an institution of higher education and then returned to complete their education. The participants were chosen from one public and one private four-year university located in the southeastern region of the United States. All of the participants maintained either full-time or part-time employment and were enrolled in their respective institution as full-time students.

Data for this study were collected through face-to-face, one-hour-long semistructured interviews. Pseudonyms were assigned to each of the participants to protect their identities. Any similarity to actual people or other organizations is purely coincidental. All interviews were tape-recorded and transcribed verbatim. The constant comparative method of data analysis was employed. This process allowed the researchers to collect rich and descriptive information.

Findings

Despite the limitation that the study findings cannot be generalized to the population of Black men who return to higher education across the United States, the two emergent themes—barriers to reentry and sources of support—affirm the researchers' position that greater attention to the experiences of the adult reentry Black male student is warranted.

Barriers. The participants identified major barriers to reentry to include their lack of understanding of the financial resources available to them, a lack of role models, and uncertainty of how to manage work–life balance.

Role Models. The role models for many reentry Black males come from those closest to them, fathers and grandfathers as well as their mothers and grandmothers. For others, the role models are Black male teachers or professors from high school and college. One respondent spoke specifically about the lack of role models in his life who could demonstrate the value and importance of getting an education. He stated:

> I only had my father as a role model. My father didn't finish high school and believed that if you worked hard education wasn't needed. Back in the day education wasn't a priority. You had to work to support your family.

Another respondent said:

> My grandfather was the stable male in my life. He did not just play the role of a grandfather who was always there, but the surrogate father. He was the one who always showed up at my basketball and football games. He was the one who taught me how to fish. He was the one who nurtured and mentored me into becoming a responsible young man.... My world collapsed when he passed away.

Financial Resources. One of the critical issues faced by reentry Black males is the burden of paying for college. Understanding how to access grants and college loans can be a daunting affair, even for those who are familiar with the process. Reentry Black males who may be the first in their family to attend college must often be guided through the financial aid maze (Harper & Griffin, 2011). The funding of appropriate amounts and types of financial aid for the Black male population is imperative to the enrollment, persistence, and graduation rates in higher education (Johnson-Ahorlua, 2012). Timothy commented about the financial barrier he encountered:

> Well, financially, I kind of overestimated my income and I thought it was going to be simple to come in. Initially, when I came in, it was not too bad because I got a lot of grants and loans.... I think I was only able to take seven or eight credits, but then eventually I worked my way up to the sophomore status.... Early junior status, the money started rolling in, but the obstacles were mostly financial.

Similarly, Mike shared:

> I didn't know where to start, and I had no knowledge of the availability of funds for people like me, older adults returning to school. At the time I returned to school, I had a job, but it wasn't the most rewarding job. My wife and I made a tough decision for me to quit my job to go to school full-time. This meant a

significant reduction in income supporting my family with my wife being a stay at home parent who is in school as well.

Other similarities surfaced during the participants' reflections on their experience of reentry, which centered on inadequate academic and career advisement, uncertainty of how to navigate through college, and insecurity with use of technology. One participant pointed out, "Although I am pleased with the academic advisement I have and continue to receive, I am not satisfied with the career advisement..."

Managing Work–Life Balance. The challenges of managing multiple roles such as spouse/partner, parent, and part-time or full-time worker are *not* unfamiliar to many adult learners. Work–life balance was cited as a major factor affecting adult learners' decision to return to and remain in school (Kasworm, 2010). For example, Scott's comment addressed this factor:

> Before I returned to school, I felt like work as a self-employed person would be an obstacle to returning to school, but the desire was there. I believed that the time that I am at school may take away from my family and business. I also feared failing school. I really felt like it would have been difficult for me to balance work, family, and school. I have the pressure of my nagging wife who is asking me how I can squeeze in work, school, and family. It's not that she doesn't support me going to school, but she was concerned about how I could manage all of my responsibilities.

Sources of Support. The participants of this study identified major sources of support to include faith/spirituality, familial support, a personal desire to serve as a role model for family and children, and an intrinsic motivation to improve themselves professionally and economically. For example, one respondent explained how family and finances influenced his decision to return to school. Kelly stated:

> Family...family and finances...I wanna be able to open a business, buy property in this lifetime, sooner than later.... My grandmother passed away two years ago (I was emotional) from lymphoma and she begged me...I tell people she asked me...but she begged me to make sure I go back to college. I had spent a year in college in 1998. In May of '98 she got diagnosed with cancer and so I took the time off and so a year later she was gone. It was traumatic for the family.... But I remember about four months before she died, when she was still speaking, she begged me to go back to college...and my mother recently got sick and I had to move back home and help take care of her.

Kelly further reflected:

> My mother had a full scholarship to college in 1974 and she spent a couple of years in school and got discouraged because it was a predominantly White

institution and she did not have the encouragement from her father and mother to go back. Now, at 55, when I hear how she speaks of her regrets and she is so disappointed that all she did was raise kids, I feel obligated to make sure her sacrifice for me...isn't in vain...I wanna be able to not only help my mother in her later years, but to also help myself...I know that my education will be key to me because I am smart. I talk well. I know I can network and I can do all this. A lot of people started businesses without degrees but for what I wanna do in life I know those credentials are going to help me because they do make a difference.

Similarly, John spoke of how his children influenced him to return to school:

Well, I look at my life and realized that I wanted to show my three boys that they must get a good education and that will require them staying in school and going to college. Basically I want to be a good role model for my children about the importance of education and I can see that they have benefited from me being in college.

Overall, when the participants were asked what their respective schools could do to help them complete their degree programs, three main strategies emerged that are consistent with Spradley's (2001) research on reentry adult Black males. The strategies include: (a) peer support in classes as an incentive for learning, such as learning support groups, the sharing of notes, and peer study sessions; (b) faculty–student relationships where the student feels that faculty members are treating him fairly and recognize the life circumstances he brings with him to class as a Black adult student; and (c) extracurricular activities for which the student finds ways to volunteer and give back as a way to connect the application of learning to community involvement (Adult College Completion Network, 2012; Quimby & O'Brien, 2006; Spradley, 2001). These strategies can provide administrators with information needed to guide the design of programs and activities to help support this population.

Conclusion and Implications for Further Research

There is an alarming downward trend in the number of Black male college students who enroll and graduate from college (JBHE, 2013). From our study and from existing research on this topic, we understand that in order for Black males to be successful in college as traditional and nontraditional students, higher education institutions must institutionalize a comprehensive approach to supporting this population's social and academic needs (Brooks, Jones, & Burt, 2012; Hill & Boes, 2013). This approach involves the variables listed in Table 6.1. Institutional recommendations for each variable are provided.

College administrators, educators, policy makers, and others who are involved in educating Black males from K–12 through postsecondary education

Table 6.1. Higher Education Initiatives in Support of Adult Black Male Academic Success

Variables	Institutional Recommendations
Cultural/social integration initiatives	Establish culturally based student development programs and services to foster a positive social environment. Sample campus programs/activities include: • Brother2Brother peer groups • Fraternal organizations • Community outreach • Retention programs • Learning communities
Mentoring programs	Facilitate ongoing mentoring support immediately upon enrollment. Sample programs with an emphasis on mentoring Black male college students include: • Faculty–Student Mentoring Program (Madison College) • The Student African Brotherhood Program (national program) • The Black Male Initiative (Tennessee State University) • African American Male Initiative (University System of Georgia)
Academic support services	Develop and implement a comprehensive student first-year program requiring a strong commitment from leaders, faculty, and staff. Sample services include: • TRIO programs • Proactive and personalized academic advising • Early academic progress/warning monitoring • Academic/social support groups • Tutorial programs
Institutional responsibility	Disaggregate institutional data to gain a better understanding of the Black male experience. Establish policy. Support diversity-based programs and services. Develop and nurture retention programs geared toward recruiting and retaining Black males. Create social networking groups.
Faculty and staff training	Institute culturally centered curricula. Foster and reward culturally responsive educators. Provide exposure to Black faculty and community leaders. Explore complex set of issues confronting Black males and education.

Sources: American Association of State Colleges and Universities (2006), Kazis et al. (2007), and Howard (2013).

must understand the importance of these variables when it comes to the educational success of reentry adult Black males and Black male college students in general. The fact that there is an increase in the number of Black males of age 25 and older returning to higher education warrants greater attention by educational institutions. These institutions must find ways to adapt to a changing clientele and then design their programs to address the special needs of this population.

References

Adult College Completion Network. (2012, August). *Strategies for success: Promising ideas in adult college completion.* Retrieved from http://www.wiche.edu/info/publications/accnPolEx-strategies-for-success.pdf

American Association of State Colleges and Universities. (2006). *Graduation rates and student success squaring means and ends.* Retrieved from http://www.aascu.org/uploadedFiles/AASCU/Content/Root/PolicyAndAdvocacy/PolicyPublications/06b_perspectives(1).pdf

Aslanian, C. (2001). You're never too old: Excerpts from adult students today. *Community College Journal, 71*(5), 56–58.

Battle, J., Alderman-Swain, W., & Tyner, A. R. (2005). Using an intersectionality model to explain the educational outcomes for Black students in a variety of family configurations. *Race, Gender & Class, 12*(1), 126–151.

Brooks, M., Jones, C., & Burt, I. (2012). Are African American males undergraduate retention programs successful? An evaluation of an undergraduate African American male retention program. *Journal of African American Studies, 17*(2), 206. doi:10.1007/s12111-012-9233-2

Census Bureau of Labor Statistics. (2010). *Back to college.* Retrieved from http://www.bls.gov/spotlight/2010/college/

Coker, A. (2003). African-American female adult learners: Motivations, challenges and coping strategies. *Journal of Black Studies, 33*, 654–674.

Cuyjet, M. J. (1997). African American men on college campuses: Their needs and their perceptions. In M. J. Cuyjet (Ed.), *New Directions for Student Services: No. 80. Helping African American men succeed in college* (pp. 5–16). San Francisco, CA: Jossey-Bass.

Cuyjet, M. J. (Ed.). (2006). *African American men in college.* San Francisco, CA: Jossey-Bass.

Denzin, N. K. (1989). *Interpretive interactionism.* Newbury Park, CA: Sage.

Duncan, G. J., & Magnuson, K. (2005). Can family socio-economic resources account for racial and ethnic test score gaps? *Future of Children, 15*, 35–54.

Fryer, R. G., & Levitt, S. D. (2006). The Black–White test score gap through third grade. *American Law and Economics Review, 8*, 249–281.

Gast, A. (2013). Current trends in adult degree programs: How public universities respond to the needs of adult learners. In R. G. White & F. R. DiSilvestro (Eds.), *New Directions for Adult and Continuing Education: No. 140. Continuing education in colleges and universities: Challenges and opportunities* (pp. 17–25). San Francisco, CA: Jossey-Bass. doi:10.1002/ace.20070

Grummon, P. T. H. (2009). Trends in higher education, *6*(1), 1–10. Retrieved from Society for College and University Planning website: http://www.scup.org/asset/53017/SCUP_TrendsWeb_v6n1.pdf

Harper, S. R. (2012). *Bibliography on Black undergraduate men: Books, reports, and peer-reviewed journal articles.* Philadelphia: University of Pennsylvania, Center for the Study of Race and Equity in Education.

Harper, S. R., & Griffin, K. A. (2011). Opportunity beyond affirmative action: How low-income and working-class Black male achievers access highly selective, high-cost colleges and universities. *Harvard Journal of African American Public Policy, 17,* 43–60.

Harper, S. R., & Harris, F. (2012). *Men of color: A role for policymakers in improving the status of Black male students in U.S. higher education.* Retrieved from https://www.gse.upenn.edu/equity/sites/gse.upenn.edu.equity/files/publications/harper_harris_2012.pdf

Hauptman, A. (2008). Participation, persistence, and attainment rates: The U.S. standing. *International Higher Education, 52,* 19–21.

Hill, C. T., & Boes, S. R. (2013). An examination of the perceived needs and satisfaction of African American Male Initiative Learning Community participants at a southeastern University. *Journal of African American Males in Education, 4*(1), 38–61.

Howard, T. C. (2013). *Black male(d). Perils and promise in the education of African American males.* New York, NY: Teachers College Press.

Hucks, D. C. (2011). New visions of collective achievement: The cross-generational schooling experiences of African American males. *The Journal of Negro Education, 80*(3), 339–357.

Johnson-Ahorlua, R. N. (2012). The academic opportunity gap: How racism and stereotypes disrupt the education of African American undergraduates. *Race Ethnicity and Education, 15*(5), 633–652. doi:10.1080/13613324.2011.645566

Johnson-Bailey, J. (2001). *Sistahs in college: Making a way out of no way.* Malabar, FL: Krieger Press.

Journal of Blacks in Higher Education (JBHE). (2013, December 8). *Black student college graduation rates remain low, but modest progress begins to show.* Retrieved from http://www.jbhe.com/features/50_blackstudent_gradrates.html

Kasworm, C. E. (2002). African American adult undergraduates: Differing cultural realities. *Journal of Continuing Higher Education, 50*(1), 10–29.

Kasworm, C. E. (2003). Setting the stage: Adults in higher education. In D. Kilgore & P. J. Rice (Eds.), *New Directions for Student Services: No. 102. Meeting the special needs of adult students* (pp. 3–10). San Francisco, CA: Jossey-Bass.

Kasworm, C. E. (2010). Adult learners in a research university: Negotiating an undergraduate student identity. *Adult Education Quarterly, 60*(2), 143–160.

Kazis, R., Callahan, A., Davidson, C., McLeod, A., Bosworth, R., Choitz, V., & Hoops, J. (2007). *Adult learners in higher education: Barriers to success and strategies.* Employment and Training Administration Occasional Paper 2007-03. Retrieved from http://files.eric.ed.gov/fulltext/ED497801.pdf

Ladson-Billings, G. (1998). Just what is critical race theory and what's it doing in a nice field like education? *Qualitative Studies in Education, 11*(1), 7–24.

Levy, Y. (2007). Comparing dropouts and persistence in e-learning courses. *Computers & Education, 48,* 185–204.

Merriam, S. (1998). What is qualitative research? *Qualitative research and case study applications in education* (Rev. ed.). San Francisco, CA: Jossey-Bass.

Park, J. H., & Choi, H. J. (2009). Factors influencing adult learners' decision to drop out or persist in online learning. *Educational Technology & Society, 12*(4), 207–217.

Quimby, J. L., & O'Brien, K. M. (2006). Predictors of well-being among nontraditional students with children. *Journal of Counseling and Development, 84*(4), 451–460.

Ross-Gordon, J. M. (2005). The adult learner of color: An overlooked college student population. *The Journal of Continuing Higher Education, 53*(2), 2–11.

Ross-Gordon, J. M., & Brown-Haywood, F. (2000). Keys to college success as seen through the eyes of African American adult students. *The Journal of Continuing Higher Education, 48*(3), 14–23.

Schott Foundation for Public Education. (2012). *The urgency of now: The Schott 50 state report on public education and Black males.* Retrieved from http://www.schottfoundation.org/urgency-of-now.pdf

Sealey-Ruiz, Y. (2007). Rising above reality: The voices of reentry Black mothers and their daughters. *The Journal of Negro Education, 76*(2), 141–153.

Southern Region Education Board (SREB). (2010). *A smart move in tough times: How SREB states can strengthen adult learning and the work force.* Retrieved from http://publications.sreb.org/2010/10E06_Smart_Move.pdf

Spradley, P. (2001). *Strategies for educating the adult Black male in college.* Retrieved from ERIC database. (ED464524)

Strauss, A., & Corbin, J. (1993). *Basics of qualitative research.* London, UK: Sage.

Strayhorn, T. (2008). The role of supportive relationships in supporting African American males in college. *NASPA Journal, 45,* 26–48.

Tyler-Smith, K. (2006). Early attrition among first time eLearners: A review of factors that contribute to drop-out, withdrawal and non-completion rates of adult learners undertaking eLearning Programmes. *Journal of Online Learning and Teaching.* Retrieved from http://jolt.merlot.org/Vol2_No2_TylerSmith.htm

Wood, J. L. (2011). Falling through the cracks. *Diverse: Issues in Higher Education, 28*(18), 24.

DIONNE ROSSER-MIMS is an associate professor of adult education and assistant division chair of education at Troy University.

GLENN A. PALMER is a professor of human resources at DeVry University.

PAMELA HARROFF is an associate dean at DeVry University.

7

This chapter addresses the challenges facing men of color who return to adult education after incarceration. It frames their experience as a war from a sociopolitical and cultural context, and then explains the support men need to succeed both in and outside the classroom.

Returning to School After Incarceration: Policy, Prisoners, and the Classroom

Brian Miller, Joserichsen Mondesir, Timothy Stater, Joni Schwartz

> There is a war between the rich and the poor, a war between the man and the woman. There is a war between the ones who say there is a war and the ones who say there isn't.
>
> —Leonard Cohen (1974)
> Reprinted by permission from Various Positions 1984 and Stranger Music 1993.

War is hell, and war seems an appropriate metaphor for the depressing state of formerly incarcerated men of color who return to adult education. These men might be called the collateral damage of a war caused by history and failed policies. They continue to be punished by barriers to reentry into society and education. Men who have been incarcerated need strong support to rebuild their lives; if denied education, they will become recidivists, not necessarily by choice, but because they cannot adjust to society.

In preparation for writing this chapter, the authors completed archival research, informally talked with men of color who were navigating the complicated minefield of the American educational system, and also drew on their own experiences. We considered three factors that determine the impact of the drug war on men of color and their access to education: past and current policies of the war on drugs, the effects of these federal policies, and reentry into the classroom experienced by those exiting the detention system and entering and/or returning to school.

Thanks to LaGuardia Community College Student Government Association (SGA), LaGuardia and Wagner Archives, and the Fortune Society for support in the writing of this chapter.

As you reflect on our participants' experiences and thoughts, connect their voices to those of your own students and their struggle to find a classroom climate that is secure and affirming (Schwartz, 2014). Ponder as well your role in the war and in their lives.

Past and Present Policies: A War of Sorts

The war on drug policies continues to depress the economic, social, and educational outcomes of men of color, who are overwhelmingly the victims and targets of these policies (vanden Heuvel, 2012). While the war on drugs is not an actual war, law enforcement tactics produce real casualties: prisoners. Since its inception in 1961, 45 million people have been arrested (National Association for the Advancement of Colored People [NAACP], 2013). The effects of these arrests are lasting; the ripples affect both the arrestee and his community.

U.S. Bureau of Justice Statistics (BJS) defines drug abuse violations as state and/or local offenses relating to the unlawful possession, sale, use, growing, manufacturing, and making of narcotic drugs including opium or cocaine and their derivatives—marijuana being one of the derivatives (BJS, Office of Justice Programs, 2013). Drug laws were designed to disrupt the flow of drugs to the United States; however, more than four fifths of drug law violation arrests are for possession (BJS, Office of Justice Programs, 2013), not for trafficking or manufacturing. Taxpayers spend 70 billion dollars per year on corrections and incarceration, culminating in a price tag of one trillion dollars over the past 40 years.

In addition, this war is fought in certain neighborhoods, particularly neighborhoods of lower socioeconomic status, not in places like Wall Street, where possession of drugs is also reported to be high (Alexander, 2010). It is not surprising, but no less troubling, that a study by the Sentencing Project and NAACP (2013) found that 38% of all people arrested on drug charges are African American. Of the 2.3 million people currently incarcerated, 25% are incarcerated for drug offenses, mainly possession, and in many cases for possession of marijuana (BJS, Office of Justice Programs, 2013).

Historically, presidents have used rhetoric to underscore their political interest or the interest of the constituents they represent, and it was President Nixon who initiated the language of war into the public conversation relating to the "war on drugs." Ronald Reagan would later add a heightened sense of urgency, declaring illegal drugs a threat to national security. In 1996, President Bill Clinton appointed an actual military general, Barry McCarthy, to the position of director of the Office of National Drug Control Policy (Associated Press, 2010). President Clinton did not select someone who understood the complexities and sensitivities of drug use in this country. Instead he chose a man of war, a choice that reflected both his views on drug control and those of a large swath of the population who elected him. It is tempting but fallacious to see the war on drugs as an earnest attempt to curb the flow and the use of drugs. Drug control policies indicate that there was and is a war on men of color, particularly in poor urban neighborhoods (Alexander, 2010).

These policies and arrests resulted in the disruption of education for large numbers of men of color and the destabilization of their families. The welfare ban on drug felons is one example. In 1996, President Clinton signed into law the Temporary Assistance for Needy Families (TANF), a program that replaced the Aid to Families with Dependent Children (AFDC). The new program changed the amount of financial assistance available to formerly incarcerated individuals who have been convicted of drug crimes. The Welfare Reform Act of 1996 (Section 115) states that persons convicted of a state or federal felony offense for using or selling drugs are subject to a lifetime ban on receiving cash assistance and food stamps. No other offenses result in losing benefits (Allard, 2002). These policies seem targeted at those who need the most help.

Today, this ideology seems to remain, but the words have changed. President Obama's 2013 budget proposed cutting services and assistance for formerly incarcerated individuals. The budget did not include federal housing mandates, giving states discretion to decide the level of assistance. In addition, there are federal bans to Supplemental Nutrition Assistance Program (SNAP), which affect the formerly incarcerated individual and his family. Such adverse policies extend as well to federal funding for school-related expenses and restrict federal aid to anyone who has been incarcerated, on probation, on parole, or residing in a halfway house (U.S. Department of Education, 2013).

These restrictions encourage recidivism by limiting options and support, effectively forcing young men of color into the underground economy. Consider the experience of a man we will call (pseudonym) Jah:

> I ended up doing dirt kuz I ain't have no choice. It was either I hustle 'n feed my kids, or I try to go back to school and hope the system feed me 'n my kids! That ain't no life. So, I made a choice—the wrong choice, I know, but I did what I felt was best. Then I got caught. Now I'm a felon and it's almost impossible to get a legal gig. Now I can't get a job or help.

Jah's experience is common to formerly incarcerated men, particularly those newly released. They are members of communities that have lost generations of capable men to the war on drugs. A father is incarcerated, then his son.

Education is not an option for them. Whole communities of people of color view education as the White man's dream, the same communities that need to participate in the restoration of the formerly incarcerated. These men face social, mental, and economic exile promulgated by policies that stigmatize them after incarceration (Alexander, 2010). Economic and social hardships cause culture shock when an ex-prisoner reenters society and, if he can manage it, reenters school.

Culture Shock: Returning to School

Exiting the prison system is as scary as going in. The world that was left behind has changed; the formerly incarcerated individual has likely failed to change with it, having acclimated to prison culture. Being out of touch is frustrating and confusing. Trauma suffered during incarceration leaves mental and emotional scars that burden an individual returning to General Education Development (GED®) or fast-paced college classes. The pressure can make for an outright terrifying experience—culture shock.

The effects of war do not end with incarceration. Zai was incarcerated in his early twenties, leaving behind a son. He was sentenced to 25 years to life. When he entered prison, there were no iPods or cell phones. Zai lacked access to computers or other technology, and he feared that he could not participate in this new world. During incarceration Zai achieved a GED®, which he had not been able to do outside. He had never had a trade, but in prison he learned basic skills in carpentry, barbering, and manual labor. Once he was back in the community, however, Zai found that his skills were not suited to employment in the age of technology. Given his felony record and his limited training, he could not earn enough to meet minimum living expenses. Now he wants to return to school, but has neither the time nor the foundation. He initially stayed with relatives and received welfare assistance on the condition that he work 30 or more hours a week. He is granted less than $200 a month in cash and just over $200 from SNAP. He accepts any work, most of it on call, making attending school very difficult.

Obtaining a GED®. If one can manage to attend school, obtaining a GED® (or one of the other new high school equivalency exam certificates) has become a viable alternative to a high school diploma. Unfortunately, funding for GED® programs either outside or inside a correctional facility is limited (Spycher, Shkodriani, & Lee, 2012), even though research has demonstrated the efficacy of correctional education programs both in reducing recidivism and in gaining future employment (Davis, Bozick, Steele, Saunders, & Miles, 2013). Therefore, many prisoners do not have the opportunity to pursue a GED®. Although many take the initiative to educate themselves, the majority become discouraged. Upon release, numerous formerly incarcerated individuals avoid pursuing higher education through a GED® for fear of being behind socially and academically.

The location of the adult education program or college is another source of culture shock. Many former prisoners want to attend school away from home to get away from "bad blood" in their neighborhoods. Others fear for their lives and avoid their old neighborhoods altogether. Some take long bus routes or subway rides to bypass neighborhoods where gang activity makes them vulnerable. Yet, even with these fears, for the sake of their children some opt to remain near home.

Child Care and Employment. If basic needs of employment and housing are not met, it is hard to focus on school. Some students are also parents who have to feed children and, possibly, partners. Children may motivate or demotivate a pursuit for education; one parent may believe that his own education will provide his children a better life and a good example. Another may be discouraged by child care expenses and opt to focus solely on a full-time job. Formerly incarcerated parents may need jobs to pay court-mandated child support. Some GED® programs and many colleges offer employment assistance that prepares individuals with interview training, resume writing, job fairs, and searches. However, sometimes this feels like too little too late; the obstacles of housing, employment, and child care seem insurmountable.

Not Walking Alone: Advisement and Counseling in College. Counseling is different from advisement. Counseling is emotional assistance, and it is important that men have an opportunity to receive one-on-one counseling should they desire it. Something as simple as having a person to talk to, listen, and understand can make a world of difference. Friends and teachers are good to talk to, but in some cases professional help is needed. Trauma counselors are especially trained to address posttraumatic stress disorder (PTSD) and to walk the formerly incarcerated through the shock of reentry and the pains of the past.

Ex-prisoners who are working on or have obtained a GED® and want to go to college will need to negotiate academia—another new culture. Many prospective students do not know which colleges or programs are shams that will take their money while promising lofty outcomes but delivering few. These men need coaching to identify legitimate institutions. The advising process should guide GED® graduates through the process of applying for college and registering for classes (National Academic Advising Association [NACADA], 2006). Good academic advisement will help men find majors that suit them. A skilled advisor will give them purpose for the present and confidence for their future, encouraging them to stay on top of things while in college.

The formerly incarcerated will need assistance with social constraints. The penal system limits a person on "extended supervision" in what social engagements he can engage in and with whom. It is at this stage that the new culture outside of prison becomes an obstacle and counseling a requisite for success. An individual may have been released with conditions such as curfew, social restraints forbidding association with any individual who has a felony (family or other), or restrictions on travel and leaving the state. These restrictions limit academic and social flexibility for meetings with tutors, advisors, classmates, professors, or just socializing with a love interest, friend, or family member.

College and Financial Support. Contributing to the culture shock are the economic realities of entering higher education. "How will I pay for it?" is a hard question to answer. Ex-prisoners can become discouraged when they try to negotiate the maze of financial aid regulations, especially because their eligibility for federal funds may be limited by the nature of their offense (U.S. Department of Education, 2013). A financial advisor who is familiar with guidelines for financial aid to the formerly incarcerated, and who will take time to discuss options, is key to academic success for the formerly incarcerated.

After enrollment, college advisors should be aware of obstacles facing the formerly incarcerated. Many students must work as well as take classes, but a felony conviction limits or excludes the formerly incarcerated from employment (Alexander, 2010). Some colleges also require students to report criminal offenses on admission applications. Advisors need to be knowledgeable about legal rights and be able to advocate for students with potential employers and college admission officers.

A Healthy Classroom Climate

When instructors create a healthy classroom (Wood, 2010), students will be comfortable and ready to learn in an atmosphere of acceptance, respect, enthusiasm, and freedom of expression. The formerly incarcerated need to adjust to a nonhostile climate. In prison, inmates had to be alert for danger; now they have to learn new behaviors. Their old behaviors may be misunderstood.

One particular behavior found special resonance with the authors and several formerly incarcerated individuals: refusing to sit with your back facing the door or a blind eye to the exits. This acute awareness of surroundings can be misconstrued as disobedience, but is an attempt to ensure safety or to preempt a perceived attack (Schwartz, 2014).

Formerly incarcerated students may have a problem with participation because of the fear of being wrong and the need to project an image of strength that protected them in prison. They may act in ways that appear awkward, absurd, guarded, or tough.

Some young men may act out when they sense a disparity in their level of skills compared to other students. They do not lack intelligence; they are trying to comprehend what is being taught. In addition, the formerly incarcerated are often older than the other students; this age disparity is an additional barrier to fitting in. Their prison experiences plus the age difference make it a challenge to relate to students just out of high school. The formerly incarcerated would be considered highly nontraditional students who experience a great degree of both cultural incongruence and dissonance (Ross-Gordon, 2005) upon entering academic environments.

An instructor needs to find creative solutions to bridge disparities between prison and school behavior. The classroom climate, coupled with the instructor's zeal for his craft along with compassion, helps the formerly incarcerated to engage while still challenging them at their current level. Schwartz (2014), in her research on engagement of young men of color in GED® programs, calls the creation of these classroom climates a type of counter-space. This effort is anything but easy, but the reward is great.

Gender of Instructors. An instructor may have difficulty understanding a formerly incarcerated student who brings prison defenses to the classroom. Research by Einarsson & Granström (2002) and Rodriguez (2002) explores the relationship between the gender of the teacher and its impact on student engagement. However, there is less research on how the gender of an adult educator may affect some formerly incarcerated males. It is the view of the authors that male instructors may be perceived as possible threats, due to a learner's previous interactions with male police officers, prison guards, and inmates. Poverty-stricken environments are frequently like police states, and males tend to respond with aggression. The same scenario applies in prison. Prisoners who are respected are not harmed. Showing innocence and submissiveness will cause problems. Male students will not feel so threatened by female instructors.

Structure and Support in the Classroom. A class with clear expectations and goals will provide necessary structure. Men coming from prison, a very predictable, extremely structured, and controlled space, need structure in their lives. Establishing a code of behavior is effective classroom management. Being able to recognize the effort of the students and praising them is important for a student's progress. This is true of all students but, again, particularly for the formerly incarcerated. Learners should not be judged for a wrong answer. Making it known that it's fine to participate without being right is an effective way of learning, especially for the struggling or guarded student. Being able to use affirmation in the class creates a great environment. Words matter. Positive language promotes respect. Respecting classmates' opinions and ideas serves to motivate and creates a classroom where students and teacher agree to put their egos to the side and to accept constructive criticism.

Relationship is key. Many young men do not have individual counselors with whom they can discuss their trials around reengagement in school. In this case, the instructor becomes the counselor; there is no better way to create a deep connection with your student than an individual private session after class. This will formulate a sense of trust. Mentors and supportive relationships with faculty are crucial for many nontraditional students (Kasworm, 2002) and even more so for the formerly incarcerated.

Peers can become another support system. Adult educators can incorporate group work so that classmates can form connections that resonate with being a family. For former gang members, a new family system is essential.

Prison inmates often turn to reading to keep occupied. Reading gives inmates the opportunity to find out their history, to understand the justice system, and, most of all, to learn about who they are as individuals. Adult educators can build on that habit developed in prison by encouraging learners to continue to structure their days with time for reading. Time can be carved out in the classroom for quiet and solitary reading.

Meaningful Curriculum. Some formerly incarcerated males choose not to attend higher learning after completing a GED® or high school. One such young man explained his choice this way: "Some may say the lack of funding is the reason for not further pursuing an education, but in my situation it was both the lack of funding and my dislike with the current curriculum, which is geared to Eurocentric concepts." When it comes to the teaching of history, minorities generally find themselves marginalized. Not everyone has this view, but it does raise the point of how important it is to have a relevant curriculum for students to apply to life outside of school (Ladson-Billings, 1994; Ross-Gordon, 1998; Ross-Gordon & Brown-Haywood, 2000).

The War Continues: The Battle Can Be Won

Leonard Cohen (1974), the Canadian singer-songwriter, declared that "There is a war between the rich and the poor.... There is a war between the ones who say there is a war and the ones who say there isn't" (verse 1). In our current educational system, the poor are often minorities and are the victims of the war on drugs and the policies associated with it. Meanwhile, those who benefit from the policies (or are unaffected by them) either do not know there is a war or support it. This reality prompts first an acknowledgment of the war, its policies, and its casualties. Then the work toward a resolution can begin. There is no better starting point than the classroom, with support from the community and commitment from the individual. The process of healing is largely in the hands of the instructors who reeducate these individuals to find their place in society.

Educators who understand the signs and symptoms of culture shock in formerly incarcerated men will be able to assure them that they are not victims, but plausible future presidents. Ultimately, it is the adult educator who can impart the knowledge that is necessary to secure a lasting future and the greatest chance for success. Adult education programs can acknowledge the needs of formerly incarcerated students, not to give them special treatment, but to minimize the effects of culture shock. Formerly incarcerated men have been through war and back. Before these eager minds can excel in the classroom, they have to survive to make it there. For this, the war must end and policies must change.

References

Alexander, M. (2010). *The new Jim Crow: Mass incarceration in the age of colorblindness*. New York, NY: New Press.
Allard, P. (2002). *Life sentences: Denying welfare benefits to women convicted of drug offenses*. Washington, DC: The Sentencing Project.
Associated Press. (2010). *AP IMPACT: After 40 years, $1 trillion, US war on drugs has failed to meet any of its goals*. Retrieved from http://www.foxnews.com/world/2010/05/13/ap-impact-years-trillion-war-drugs-failed-meet-goals/
Bureau of Justice Statistics (BJS), Office of Justice Programs. (2013). *Drugs and crime facts*. Retrieved from http://www.bjs.gov/content/dcf/enforce.cfm
Cohen, L. (1974). There is a war. On *New skin for the old ceremony* [CD]. New York, NY: Columbia Records.
Davis, L., Bozick, R., Steele, J., Saunders, J., & Miles, J. (2013). *Evaluating the effectiveness of correctional education*. Prepared for the Department of Justice. Retrieved from www.bja.gov/Publications/RAND_Correctional-Education-Meta-Analysis.pdf
Einarsson, C., & Granström, K. (2002). Gender-biased interaction in the classroom: The influence of gender and age in the relationship between teacher and pupil. *Scandinavian Journal of Educational Research, 46*, 117–127.

Kasworm, C. (2002). African American adult undergraduates: Differing cultural realities. *The Journal of Continuing Higher Education, 50*(1), 10–20.

Ladson-Billings, G. (1994). *The dreamkeepers: Successful teaching for African-American students.* San Francisco, CA: Jossey-Bass.

National Academic Advising Association (NACADA). (2006). *Concept of academic advising.* Retrieved from http://www.nacada.ksu.edu/Resources/Clearinghouse/View-Articles/Concept-of-Academic-Advising-a598.aspx

National Association for the Advancement of Colored People (NAACP). (2013). *Criminal justice fact sheet.* Retrieved from http://www.naacp.org/pages/criminal-justice-fact-sheet

Rodriguez, N. (2002). *Gender differences in disciplinary approaches.* Retrieved from ERIC database. (ED468259)

Ross-Gordon, J. M. (1998). Investigating the needs, concerns, and utilization of services reported by minority adults at "Eastern University." *The Journal of Continuing Higher Education, 46*(3), 21–33.

Ross-Gordon, J. M. (2005). The adult learner of color: An overlooked college student population. *The Journal of Continuing Higher Education, 53*(2), 2–11.

Ross-Gordon, J. M., & Brown-Haywood, F. (2000). Keys to college success as seen through the eyes of African American adult students. *The Journal of Continuing Higher Education, 48*(3), 14–23.

Schwartz, J. (2014). Classrooms of spatial justice: Counter-spaces and young men of color in a GED® program. *Adult Education Quarterly, 64*(2), 110–127.

Spycher, D., Shkodriani, G., & Lee, J. (2012). *The other pipeline: From prison to diploma.* Prepared for the College Board Advocacy and Policy Center. Washington, DC. Retrieved from youngmenofcolor.collegeboard.org

U.S. Department of Education. (2013). *Federal student aid. Incarcerated individuals and eligibility for federal student aid.* Retrieved from https://studentaid.ed.gov/sites/default/files/aid-info-for-incarcerated-individuals.pdf

vanden Heuvel, K. (2012, November 20). It's time to end the war on drugs [The Nation]. http://www.thenation.com/blog/171383/its-time-end-war-drugs

Welfare Reform Act of 1996 § 115, 42 U.S.C. § 1305. (1996). Personal Responsibility and Work Opportunity Reconciliation Act of 1996. Pub. L. No. 104–193, 110 Stat. 2105.

Wood, J. (2010). *Communication mosaics: An introduction to the field of communication.* Independence, KY: Cengage.

BRIAN MILLER is a recent graduate of LaGuardia Community College and program outreach coordinator for the Black Male Empowerment Cooperative (BMEC) Program at LaGuardia.

JOSERICHSEN MONDESIR is currently a student at LaGuardia Community College majoring in secondary education.

TIMOTHY STATER is currently a student at Brooklyn College majoring in business and communication.

JONI SCHWARTZ is an associate professor in the Humanities Department at LaGuardia Community College, City University of New York.

8

> The 2008 GI Bill offers college funds for veterans. Yet Black male vets are not taking advantage of these benefits. This chapter examines personal and societal problems that hinder access to higher education for Black vets, and suggests some ways adult educators can advocate for these young men.

Empty Promise: Black American Veterans and the New GI Bill

Alford H. Ottley

If someone falls in a pit and a ladder is let down to rescue him, but the distance between the rungs is too great to climb from one to the next, then the ladder is of little use to the victim of the pit. If funds for education are available to the returning vet but there are barriers (access) and obstacles (readiness) to utilizing those funds, then they are of little use to those who may be eligible for such funds. The Post-9/11 Veterans Educational Assistance Act of 2008 expanded the educational benefits for military veterans who have served since September 11, 2001. The law provides for veterans' college expenses and allows funding for 100% of a public four-year undergraduate education to a veteran who has served three years on active duty since September 11, 2001. There are also provisions for the veteran to transfer educational benefits to a spouse or children after serving or agreeing to serve for 10 years.

Yet, by all measures, Black American returning vets are not utilizing these benefits as much as White or Asian Americans. The question is why? Are there deliberate and sustained institutional efforts to deny access to GI educational benefits to Black vets? Are there situational or societal barriers impeding access to educational benefits for Black vets? This chapter raises those questions in an effort to come to grips with the apparent disparities in the use of the new GI Bill by Black male vets.

The Black Male Returning Serviceman

The needs of Black veterans are similar to those of any veteran, but the severity of the need and the traumatic effect that denial of service creates are considerably greater in the case of Black veterans. All veterans need access to adequate housing, quality healthcare, tertiary education, and sustainable employment, but among Black veterans both the need and benefit are generational. Access to essentials becomes a new method of ascription for Black veterans. Unencumbered access to healthcare, adult education, employment, and familial support would substantially alter the circumstances and even the destiny of the Black vet. These necessities are generally not found in abundance within the neighborhoods to which the Black vet will likely return. Access to higher education, especially adult education, is paramount to the returning Black servicemen for societal mobility and general wellness as they reintegrate into their community.

Although this chapter will reference other necessities of well-being, such as healthcare, employment, and housing, the emphasis is on education, since education can facilitate other necessities. Because, as documented later in the chapter, Black returning vets are utilizing GI benefits less than other ethnic groups, and because there are so few longitudinal studies addressing the "why" of this phenomenon, conclusions will be drawn on anecdotal data from the experience of returning veterans, principally from the Gulf, Afghanistan, and Iraq wars.

Higher education of all types (adult secondary [GED], college/university, vocational, etc.) remains an avenue to self-improvement and economic stability. Adult education has become one of the only ways a Black veteran can even begin to make a sustainable change to his and his family's socioeconomic status (SES). However, the cost of tertiary education in the United States has increased each year, even in years when the median household income did not keep pace with education costs. College tuition has become less and less affordable, even with the assistance of the GI Bill and financial aid. Veterans, and especially Black veterans, are often unable to borrow additional funds for education due to limited resources and discriminatory lending practices.

Nevertheless education, formal and informal, is not the only situational/social barrier the returning Black vet will face. While education in its broadest sense can facilitate and mitigate other barriers, the returning Black vet will likely face other barriers, such as adequate access to healthcare, employment, and housing. Access to quality healthcare is essential for all returning vets and is pivotal to reintegration into the community. Quality healthcare is a function of many factors including, but not limited to, the quality of the staff, the ratio of professional staff to patient load, the timely access to diagnostic equipment, and the stability and adequacy of funding. A demographic report by the U.S. Department of Defense (2012) showed that 16.9% of the active-duty military population is Black. The aggregate SES of this subgroup of the military population is lower in comparison to other demographic groups within the military with the exception of the Hispanic subgroup. A lower SES probably means a greater likelihood that Black servicemen when discharged will return to the neighborhoods from which they came. These areas historically have diminished access to quality healthcare and/or have insufficient quality facilities to serve the needs of their community.

Employment is also vital to the welfare of the returning vet. There was a time when this nation valued returning vets and coveted their skills in leadership, teamwork, resourcefulness, loyalty, reliability, and discipline. Today, amid the crisis of high unemployment, returning vets are no longer favored; rather, they receive low priority in hiring. Employers may choose candidates with only minimal attention to veterans' personal virtues and professional skills.

This nation has a long history of discrimination against Blacks, women, and other minorities in its employment (hiring) practices. Discrimination is so ingrained in the fiber of commerce that one may assert it is in the national DNA. In this depressed economy, employers may revert to old prejudices; they have their pick of hundreds, even thousands of job applicants. Hiring discrimination is alive and well. Unfortunately, there is a natural progression of not being able to find meaningful employment, not being well educated, not having strong familial support, and not having adequate healthcare. That progression leads to homelessness!

According to the U.S. Department of Housing and Urban Development (2012), in January 2012, there were 633,782 homeless persons living in America, of whom 62,619 were veterans. Further, nearly 56% of all homeless veterans are Black or Hispanic males. Lack of awareness of the VA's veteran's housing benefits coupled with a greater likelihood of mis- or underdiagnosis of mental and physical health issues are the leading reasons for this staggering percentage. Lack of employment or sporadic employment causes a myriad of other problems, not the least of which is the strain on the family unit.

All of the factors noted earlier—adequate healthcare, stable employment, and suitable housing—are basic psychological and safety needs as expressed in Maslow's hierarchy of need. Not meeting these basic needs may become a barrier to seeking and persevering in educational attainment. Yet, attaining these needs is not necessarily a function of the formal education process. Education, in fact, enables improvements in these other areas. However, "education" that informs people of the existence and location of appropriate healthcare services is not what we define as higher education; rather we call it information. "Education" that informs people of the existence, location, and availability of adequate housing is also not what we define as higher education. And "education" that informs people of the existence, location, and availability of gainful employment indeed may require some form of higher education, but is certainly not a prerequisite to obtaining gainful employment. The acquisition of relevant information to inform these needs is an education process and remains a barrier to the formal higher education process.

The GI Bill: Past and Present

"The road to hell is paved with good intentions," a parable often attributed to the French monk Saint Bernard of Clairvaux (c. 1150), may aptly apply to the history of the GI Bill. Certainly, few, if any, question the good intentions of the bill; nevertheless, the result certainly did not match the intent.

The Past. Meyer's (2011) video about the post–World War II GI Bill and Black veterans reveals overwhelming evidence of discrimination against veterans of color and non-White ethnic minorities. Following World War II and the Korean wars, segregation was still the law of the land and discrimination abounded. Following the Vietnam War, vestiges of segregation remained. Jim Crow laws were still practiced in some areas, especially south of the Mason–Dixon Line. And sufficient institutional racism made it very difficult for Blacks and other minorities to gain support. Moreover, at the close of the Vietnam War, access to veteran services by minority veterans in general became even more challenging. In a recent story about a Vietnam-era veteran who has been waiting for 43 years for the Veterans Administration (VA) to process his claim, Prine (2013) summarized the troubled history of the VA's treatment of minority veterans:

> VA officials...have publicly acknowledged that minorities and female veterans often were treated as second-class citizens by VA and other federal agencies, despite wounds, illnesses and injuries as serious as those that white GIs suffered. (para. 7–9)

In 2004, as the "War on Terror" campaign under the Bush administration steadily increased, about 700,000 military personnel engaged in some aspect of two wars. Linda Bilmes, former Assistant Secretary of Commerce in the Clinton administration, predicted that these 700,000 would eventually enter the VA system and that provision should be made for their claims (as cited in Graziano, 2012, para. 9). No provision was made. The result was that in 2006 Congress had to pass an emergency $2.7 billion supplemental package for veterans' health programs because the Bush administration's budget had substantially underestimated the number of veterans needing care. Graziano related that in spite of the emergency funding, the Bush administration still planned cutbacks to the VA in consecutive budgets.

Sorg (2007) asserted that the VA had a backlog totaling nearly 380,000 pending claims and was riddled with inconsistencies and inaccurate benefit rulings. Most damning was the admission in that article by attorney Craig Kabatchnick, the senior appellate attorney for the VA's Office of General Counsel from 1990 to 1995: "Our job was to deny claims....There was no official policy, but ranking attorneys instructed staff to fight and deny cases—even though the law mandated that they give veterans the benefit of the doubt" (as cited in Sorg, 2007, para. 7).

In 2007, Priest and Hull of *The Washington Post* published a series of articles depicting across-the-board treatment of veterans at the Walter Reed Army Medical Facility. (It should be noted that the Walter Reed Army Medical Facility was part of the Department of Defense, not the VA.) The series documented deplorable treatment, or lack thereof, of some of the most vulnerable veterans—those with severe injuries. Often, such injuries resulted in permanent disability that required filing a claim with the VA. It was the responsibility of the VA to assess these cases and, when warranted, to issue disability compensation. Because of the culture of denial of benefits, the VA often forced returning veterans into homelessness. During the Bush administration, it was estimated that there were approximately 300,000 homeless veterans in the United States (Sorg, 2007). Even when veterans were granted disability benefits, compensation was minimal, especially for those living in cities. A veteran with a disability rating of 100, indicating that he or she could not work due to injury, received only $2,400 a month.

Sorg (2007) reported that in contrast to the Bush administration, the Obama administration aggressively attacked what appeared to be a pervasive issue. With the appointment of General Eric Shinseki, himself a disabled veteran, as Secretary of Veterans Affairs, the administration sought to overhaul the VA system. There was a cultural shift within the VA from adversary to advocate. Claims adjudicators were ordered to reinstitute benefit of the doubt as the legal standard of proof. Congress passed a record budget of $112.3 billion for the VA, a $15 billion increase from the previous year. It was the largest VA budget increase in three decades and enabled more than 250,000 veterans who had lost benefits to reenroll.

At the 2012 Democratic Convention, General Shinseki spoke about his work in the Obama administration: "Since President Obama took office, nearly 800,000 veterans gained access to VA healthcare. There's been a historic expansion of treatment for PTSD and traumatic brain injury. President Obama has expanded job training to prepare vets for the jobs of the future. And we're on track to end veterans' homelessness by 2015" (Shinseki, 2012, para. 5).

The Present. There must be military and civilian recognition that the number one injury to be acknowledged and addressed is the injury to the mind induced by combat. Writing about organizations working to prevent suicide among veterans, Cantrell (2013) described how injuries have become manifest in "the staggering rate of increasing suicides among our active duty military and veterans" (para. 7). Often called silent or unseen injuries, posttraumatic stress disorder (PTSD) and traumatic brain injury (TBI) left untreated exhibit themselves in depression, anxiety, substance abuse, rage, and suicide. The existence and pervasiveness of PTSD are only now being fully acknowledged by the medical community.

Clearly, PTSD and TBI are medical factors that impede Black vets from participating in higher education until their PTSD and/or TBI is under control. Roxanne Merritt, of the Army's John F. Kennedy Special Warfare Center and School, said that emotional injuries carry a stigma: "Troops suffering from unseen injuries tell me they often find themselves ostracized or criticized for short-term memory loss, lack of or over-concentration, panic attacks, and anger management" (as cited in Quade, 2010, Sec. 2, para. 6).

Piven (2004) revealed that hundreds of servicemen were dishonorably discharged from the Army in the early part of the Iraq War for "personality disorders or another diminishing personality trait" (p. 36) that were later discovered to be misdiagnoses of PTSD. Only after years of veteran outcry have the errors been acknowledged and properly identified, albeit too late for many who suffered numerous hardships. But these misdiagnoses were across the board. They were not unique to any subgroup of the returning vet. So, how can we identify whether disparity currently exists between the Black male vet and the universe of returning vets? One would have to prove that deliberate and sustained efforts are present to deny access to VA services to Black vets.

According to historian Benjamin Fleury-Steiner (2012), there is not one singular life experience common to all Black veterans. A longitudinal study would best present a true picture of the complications Black service members faced on returning to the United States. Fleury-Steiner (2012) proposed that such a study should define the "multiple individual, institutional and structural contexts" in which Black veterans make sense of their postwar lives (p. 18). This is to say that any ethnographic researcher earnestly seeking insight into difficulties Black veterans face upon their return to the United States cannot look at one particular factor, such as the presence or absence of a male father figure in the home; rather, the entirety of the social context of a sample population of the returning Black veterans has to be examined for an accurate assessment of the plight of Black servicemen.

Implications for Adult Education

Consider the visual introduced at the beginning of the chapter, that of the pit and the ladder. If the pit is a dark place and the ladder reaches toward freedom from the pit, there must be some kind of progression from the bottom to the top. If we superimpose Maslow's hierarchy of needs on the ladder, then psychological needs precede safety needs that precede belonging needs, etc. As pointed out previously, for many returning Black vets, the instability or even the nonexistence of these basic needs hinders or precludes the returning Black vet from seeking/pursuing/persisting in adult education despite the fact that funds are available to him.

However, as also stated earlier, adult education can facilitate the acquisition of these basic needs. For adult education to effectively become a catalyst for change for the returning Black vet, it must provide three things: acclimation, information, and education.

Acclimation. There are many models that higher education uses to help acclimate the returning vet to the college, the classroom, and the community in general. One such model, the SERV Center at Cleveland State University, recognizes the difficulty the vet faces integrating back into society after the horrific experience of combat. You can take a soldier out of Iraq or Afghanistan in one day, but it often takes years to take Iraq or Afghanistan out of the soldier.

Acclimation is the process of transitioning the returning vet to the community. In an infomercial entitled "The American Veteran: Education for Returning Vets" (U.S. Department of Veterans Affairs, Office of Public and Intergovernmental Affairs, 2009), the commentator explains: "for veterans returning from combat, going back to school presents more challenges than simply learning the material in their textbooks. Sometimes sitting in the classroom itself can be a challenge..." A returning army veteran noted "noises made me uncomfortable in the classroom, unfamiliar faces and individuals I knew I could relate with made it very difficult for me to concentrate on the professor and the material being taught..."

Cleveland State University (CSU) began a program and an office called Supportive Education for the Returning Veteran (SERV). SERV is a variety of services that help the returning vet navigate the educational process from admission to graduation. The service office creates a supportive environment in which virtually every academic function is represented. Moreover, at CSU, basic classes, such as Composition I and II, have sections dedicated solely to returning vets that ease the transition.

Information. While the higher education facility may not be able to provide basic necessities such as food, housing, and healthcare, they can provide up-to-date information to, and partner with, organizations that do provide these services. The University of Northwestern at Saint Paul, for example, employs licensed counselors and partners with local counseling centers to provide additional support to students both on and off campus. The University of the District of Columbia, basically a commuter university with no student housing of its own, partnered with a nearby apartment complex to provide student housing. In the same manner, educational institutions can be fully engaged through partnership and/or by providing current information about other basic services. And, more than just providing information, there must also be an interface with the provider, preferably on campus, so that the returning vet is not bounced around from place to place. This in and of itself is an obstacle to persistence in higher education.

Education. An institution of higher education cannot assume that it is automatically equipped to meet the education needs of the returning vet. There must be recognition that the returning vet has acquired life skills that can be assessed and worthy of academic credit. One might say that an institution of higher education has a moral responsibility to determine how prior learning of the returning vet can earn academic credit.

A Council for Adult and Experiential Learning (CAEL, 2010) study, "Fueling the Race to Postsecondary Success" (para. 2), examined data on 62,475 adult students at 48 colleges and universities across the country. CAEL found that graduation rates were two and a half times higher for students with prior learning assessment (PLA) credit. Further, PLA students also had higher persistence rates and a faster time to degree completion.

One such program, New Jersey's Warren County Community College VIPER (Veterans in Pursuit of Educational Readiness) Program, enables the returning vet to earn an associate's degree in as little as one year. The Warren [County, NJ] Reporter (2013) reported that a veteran's military training may qualify for up to 34 credits, with specific career training, such as business or automotive technology, adding up to 11 more credits. A student may finish an associate's degree in one semester and transfer directly to a bachelor's program (Warren Reporter, 2013, para. 8).

There was a time in our history when high school aged Blacks were "relegated" to the trades or vocational education rather than being placed on the academic or college track. Today, many trades pay an attractive salary and require only a two-year degree. For the returning Black vet, this can mean little to no debt upon completion because of the provisions in the "New GI Bill." Further, there is a high probability of employment in high demand area, such as healthcare, technology, and electronics.

Torpey (2012) released a list from the Bureau of Labor Statistics of the 25 highest paid occupations requiring only an associate's degree. Among them were air traffic controllers ($108,040), radiation therapists ($74,980), diagnostic medical sonographers ($64,380), radiologic technologists and technicians ($54,340), and occupational therapist technicians ($51,010) (U.S. Department of Labor, Bureau of Labor Statistics, 2012). Many of the returning Black vets already have some training in several of these and other listed occupations on the top 25 list.

Conclusion

While it appears that the VA itself has recently become more of an advocate for the vet rather than an adversary, the nation itself has done little to recognize, appreciate, or celebrate the returning vet. The military today is an all-volunteer military. There is no mandatory service. Regardless of one's politics, the military and the intelligence community are constituted to keep this nation safe and strong. Black Americans comprise 16.9% of the active-duty force as compared to approximately 6.2%, or slightly less than half, of the total Black American population (U.S. Department of Defense, 2012). The Black American male has thus assumed a greater level of responsibility for the defense of this nation than his demographics would suggest.

So why is it that those who have given so much receive so little from the nation they serve? Clearly, higher education is the single most viable means by which the Black veteran can even begin to make a sustainable change to the SES of himself and his family. Are there deliberate and sustained institutional efforts to deny access to GI educational benefits to Black vets? Not really! Are there situational or societal barriers impeding access to educational benefits for Black vets? Clearly! Access impeded whether deliberate or circumstantial is clearly a barrier to reaping the benefits of the New GI Bill. Educational disadvantage started in substandard urban primary and secondary schools. It continued with a higher-than-average high school dropout rate. It was further compounded by a historically inept and highly adversarial VA administration.

We owe our service personnel a debt of gratitude, considering the true cost of their service. Veterans went into service whole and often returned broken. If the VA were truly earnest about assisting those who gave disproportionately so much, namely, Black American males, it would ensure that Black veterans are better prepared to utilize the GI Bill funds *prior* to discharge. Educational training (often remedial) required to successfully access and persist in higher education would help. Such training done during military service could be coupled with other services (emotional, physical, and environmental) that would begin the process of reacclimation to civilian life. And, once in higher education, the college or university must take a more aggressive role in assuring persistence and success by providing links to other services than educational services and awarding credit for life experiences.

References

Cantrell, B. (2013, September 19). Returning home through the eyes of our troops and their families [Blog post]. Retrieved from http://www.huffingtonpost.com/dr-bridget-cantrell/returning-home-through-th_b_3954203.html
Council for Adult and Experiential Learning (CAEL). (2010, February). *Prior learning assessment*. Retrieved from http://www.cael.org/What-We-Do/Prior-Learning-Assessment
Fleury-Steiner, B. (2012). *Disposable heroes: America's betrayal of African-American veterans.* Lanham, MD: Rowman & Littlefield.
Graziano, J. (2012, October 25). The mystifying misperception [Blog post]. Retrieved from http://www.huffingtonpost.com/joseph-graziano/returning-veterans-_b_2017297.html
Meyer, G. (2011, June 2). The effect of the GI Bill on African Americans: How did the GI Bill impact the education and success of post WWII African Americans veterans [Video file]. Retrieved from http://prezi.com/itat9o8ln7ib/the-effect-of-the-gi-bill-on-african-americans/
Piven, F. F. (2004). *The war at home: The domestic cost of Bush's militarism.* New York, NY: The New Press.
Post-9/11 Veterans Educational Assistance Act. (2008). U.S.C. Chapter 33 Sec. 3301 *et seq.* Retrieved from http://www.law.cornell.edu/uscode/text/38/part-III/chapter-33
Priest, D., & Hull, A. (2007, February 18). Soldiers face neglect, frustration at army's top medical facility. *The Washington Post*. Retrieved from http://www.washingtonpost.com/wp-dyn/content/article/2007/02/17/AR2007021701172.html
Prine, C. (2013, May 26). Black vets accuse VA of unfair treatment. *Pittsburgh [PA] Tribune-Review.* Retrieved from http://triblive.com/news/allegheny/4074530-74/veterans-hill-claim#axzz2k0MwNhnf
Quade, A. (2010, November 11). Dealing with the unseen scars of war. Retrieved from http://www.cnn.com/2010/HEALTH/11/08/ptsd.military.treatment
Shinseki, E. (2012, September 5). *DNC: Remarks by Secretary of Veterans Affairs Eric Shinseki.* Transcript retrieved from http://apmobile.worldnow.com/story/19467013/dnc-remarks-by-secretary-of-veterans-affairs-eric-shinseki
Sorg, L. (2007, March 14). "The VA is waiting for us to die": A soldier battles a system stacked against him. *Indy Week.* Retrieved from http://www.indyweek.com/indyweek/the-va-is-waiting-for-us-to-die/Content?oid=1201075
Torpey, E. (2012). High wages after high school—without a bachelor's degree. *Occupational Outlook Quarterly, 56*(2), 28. Retrieved from http://www.bls.gov/opub/ooq/2012/summer/home.htm
U.S. Department of Defense. (2012). *2011 demographic profile of the military community.* Retrieved from http://www.militaryonesource.mil/12038/MOS/Reports/2011_Demographics_Report.pdf

U.S. Department of Housing and Urban Development. (2012, November). *HUD's 2012 continuum of care homeless assistance programs: Homeless populations and subpopulations.* Retrieved from https://www.onecpd.info/reports/CoC_PopSub_NatlTerrDC_2012.pdf

U.S. Department of Labor, Bureau of Labor Statistics. (2012). *Education and training outlook for occupations, 2012–22.* Retrieved from http://www.bls.gov/emp/ep_edtrain_outlook.pdf

U.S. Department of Veterans Affairs, Office of Public and Intergovernmental Affairs. (2009, January). The American veteran: Education for returning vets [Video file]. Retrieved from http://www.csuohio.edu/academic/serv/

Warren Reporter. (2013, May 4). Richard Feldman named VIPER coordinator at Warren County Community College. Retrieved from http://www.nj.com/warrenreporter/index.ssf/2013/05/richard_feldman_named_viper_co.html

ALFORD H. OTTLEY is vice president of Academic Affairs and dean of the college at Pillar College, Newark, NJ.

9 | *In this concluding chapter, the editors offer their reflections on the key themes of this volume and implications for future research and practitioners of adult education.*

Black Males and Adult Education: A Call to Action

Brendaly Drayton, Dionne Rosser-Mims, Joni Schwartz, Talmadge C. Guy

The purpose of this volume is to make space for the experiences and voices of Black men in the canon of adult education literature, to promote a critical assessment of institutional policies and practices, and to foster awareness and involvement among adult educators in pursuing the vision of a democratic society by addressing the issues of inequity and injustice. We link the past and the present, the private and the public, and the individual and the structural to show their interconnectivity and the need for multifaceted approaches to address the concerns of Black men in our schools and by extension our society.

Our purpose is not to support a social pathology perspective (Polite & Davis, 1999) of Black men but to expose the unique challenges they face in the crisis of negative perception and resulting daily lived effects that detract from their efforts to prosper. Collectively, the chapters in this volume convey the importance of understanding lived experience as a prerequisite for establishing appropriate policies and practices to meet the needs of Black male students in educational settings.

Understanding Lived Experience

As specifically discussed in the beginning chapters and foregrounded in the remaining chapters, the significance of race and gendered racism and its associated social, economic, and educational consequences is critical to understanding the relationship between the experiences of Black men and education. To understand the present, one must look to the past; therefore, many of the authors employed critical race theory (CRT) to expose the social, institutional, and economic circumstances that predispose many Black men, particularly those of low socioeconomic status, to pathways away from higher levels of education necessary for their economic and social well-being (Delgado & Stephanic, 2001).

Common barriers were identified among subgroups addressed in this volume. First, prevailing negative stereotypes as Black men are further compounded by prejudicial treatment as low-literacy persons, professionals, veterans, and formerly incarcerated that limit employment opportunities, foster alienating educational environments, and contribute to the vicious cycle of poverty from which they seek to escape. Second, minimal financial resources constrain the pursuit of higher levels of education. The increasing costs of higher education and meeting family needs are often deterrents to educational progress and social mobility. Third, impoverished communities present additional barriers to engagement in the classroom, such as limited access to information, reduced college options, inadequate college preparation, and unrecognized and untreated effects of trauma.

In drawing attention to overarching issues, we acknowledge intragroup diversity among Black men and other men of color as well as the overlapping and complex nature of their identities. We recognize that each subgroup faces particular challenges that must be addressed accordingly. The volume clearly communicates that opportunities and resources mediate between aspirations and outcomes. As a marginalized population, Black men do not reap the full benefits this society affords to its citizens. While education is not the sole means for redressing this wrong, it is a pathway for Black men to claim full participation in society. Adult educators can effectively respond to issues of access, engagement, and successful completion of academic goals through an understanding of Black men's experiences.

Implications for Future Research

A glaring omission is apparent in the adult education literature—the voices and experiences of Black males. The limited knowledge of Black men's experiences in educational settings calls for adult education researchers and practitioners to facilitate an ongoing research agenda to address the interconnection of Black men's multidimensional identities, the larger society, and the classroom. Some areas for consideration, not addressed in this volume, include the relationship between engagement in education and sexual orientation, athletics, and a marginally explored area related to the influence of social media on Black men's lives. How do Black men's experiences contribute to our understanding of these relationships? In each of these categories there are overarching stereotypes that influence how Black men are perceived and treated and that contribute to the educational choices they make.

A reoccurring theme in this volume is the harmful impact of the negative stereotyping and the pathological construction of Black male identities. Expanding research on high achievers to diverse educational settings would not only disrupt this construction but also offer strategies for overcoming difficult situations. A compilation of these strategies would provide a toolkit for Black male students to utilize and educators and policy makers to reference in constructing supportive programs. In addition, Black Americans are more likely to identify spirituality as a source of coping and strength than any other group (Walker & Dixon, 2002). More importantly, some Black masculinity models incorporate spirituality as a component of manhood (Hammond & Mattis, 2005; Jackson & Dangerfield, 2004). Consequently, more research is needed to understand the role of spirituality in Black men's engagement with education.

In this volume, we have also addressed the challenges Black men face in attaining education. An extension of this research would explore programs that are investing in the lives of young men and providing opportunities for success. There are good models in communities across the nation that have been effective for decades such as Black Male Empowerment and Initiative Programs, STEM undergraduate research programs designed for Black males, fatherhood programs, and a variety of mentoring programs. Recently, President Obama has drawn national attention to these valued resources through his 2014 My Brother's Keeper initiative. More specifically, it highlights the importance of interdisciplinary collaboration, institutional partnerships, and funding in providing access to resources that promote educational success and well-being.

Implications for Adult Educators and Adult Education Practice

In order for adult educators to understand the experiences of Black men, we must recognize the systems in place that are complicit in creating the disenfranchised conditions from which they operate. Therefore, in line with our goals to generate awareness and active involvement among adult educators in addressing the educational, and by extension, the social and economic concerns of Black men, each chapter provides practical applications to which adult educators can apply. Overwhelmingly, the authors point to the importance for adult educators to recognize the intricate relationship between the larger society and the classroom, treatment of Black male students as whole persons, and the creation and maintenance of a supportive environment.

A supportive environment involves many components, not all of which are addressed in these chapters. Nevertheless, they provide ideas to explore and build upon. First, the historically pervasive nature of the negative construction of Black male identities calls for an intentional examination of its influence on student–teacher relationships, policies, and procedures. Second, a culturally relevant pedagogy draws upon Black men's experiences as resources for fostering engagement and learning. Third, because many Black men from impoverished neighborhoods are first-time college students, they lack the social competence necessary for college life. Beyond the immediate need of financial and academic support, career guidance, mentoring, and cultural social support are needed to help students transition into and complete their educational programs.

In conclusion, what has been identified through this volume is an urgency that needs to be addressed. Educational, social, and economic disparities persist for Black males—recent research (Bal, Sullivan, & Harper, 2014; Codrington & Fairchild, 2012; Rodriguez, 2011) exposes documented cases where Black males continue to be disproportionally assigned to the special education track at a greater rate than their White male counterparts. At a larger social level, Black males are still disproportionally incarcerated at higher rates than their White male counterparts even when the crimes committed are the same (Alexander, 2010). The declining number of Black males entering higher education and the hemorrhaging of those already in the system are enough reasons for adult educators, policy makers, and concerned Americans to pay attention to these dangerous trends. Adult education can play an increasing role in serving the needs of this population.

References

Alexander, M. (2010). *The new Jim Crow: Mass incarceration in the age of colorblindness*. New York, NY: The New Press.

Bal, A., Sullivan, A., & Harper, J. (2014). A situated analysis of special education disproportionality for systemic change in an urban school district. *Remedial and Special Education, 35*, 3–14.

Codrington, J., & Fairchild, H. H. (2012). *Special education and the mis-education of African American children: A call to action*. Washington, DC: The Association of Black Psychologists.

Delgado, R., & Stephanic, J. (2001). *Critical race theory: An introduction*. New York, NY: University Press.

Hammond, W. P., & Mattis, J. S. (2005). Being a man about it: Manhood meaning among Black men [Electronic Version]. *Psychology of Men & Masculinity, 6*, 114–126.

Jackson R. L., II, & Dangerfield, C. L. (2004). Defining Black masculinity as cultural property: Toward an identity negotiation paradigm. In R. L. Jackson II (Ed.), *Black communication & identities: Essential readings* (pp. 197–208). Thousand Oaks, CA: Sage.

My Brother's Keeper. (2014). *Creating opportunities for boys and young men of color*. Retrieved from http://www.whitehouse.gov/the-press-office/2014/05/30/fact-sheet-report-opportunity-all-my-brother-s-keeper-blueprint-action

Polite, V., & Davis, J. (1999). Introduction. In V. Polite & J. Davis (Eds.), *African American males in school and society* (pp. 1–7). New York, NY: Teachers College Press.

Rodriguez, A. B. (2011). *Effects of schools attuned on special education referrals for African American boys* (Doctoral dissertation). Retrieved from ProQuest Dissertations and Theses database. (UMI No. 3413187)

Walker, K., & Dixon, V. (2002). Spirituality and academic performance among African-American college students. *Journal of Black Psychology, 28*(2), 107–121.

BRENDALY DRAYTON *earned her PhD in adult education from Pennsylvania State University.*

DIONNE ROSSER-MIMS *is an associate professor of adult education and assistant division chair of education at Troy University.*

JONI SCHWARTZ *is an associate professor in the Humanities Department at LaGuardia Community College, City University of New York.*

TALMADGE C. GUY *is an associate professor of adult education at The University of Georgia.*

Index

Acclimation, 84–85
Adames, H. Y., 8
Adult basic education and literacy (ABEL) program, 27–28; and considerations for adult educators, 33–34; findings on, 30–33; good provider, role of, 27–29, 33; independence as reason for participation in, 30–31; research design, 30; responsibility as reason for participation in, 31–33
Adult College Completion Network, 64
Affective relationships, 43. *See also* Mentoring relationship
African American male. *See* Black men
Aid to Families with Dependent Children (AFDC), 71
Alderman-Swain, W., 61
Alexander, M., 70, 71, 74, 92
Alfred, M., 53, 56, 57
Allard, P., 71
Allen, J. D., 7
Alridge, D. P., 8, 9
Ambinder, M., 20
Amott, T. L., 9
Andersen, M., 16, 23
Anderson, A., 27
Anderson, E., 29
Anderson, J., 27, 34
Anderson, T., 34
Andrews-Guillen, C., 7
Antigonish Movement, 40
Armentano, P., 70
Aslanian, C., 61
Astin, A. W., 43
Autonomy, 31

Bal, A., 91
Barton, D., 28
Bartowski, J., 28
Battle, J., 61
Baumgartner, L. M., 6
Beal, F. M., 8
Beder, H., 32
Bell, D. A., Jr., 6
Bernard, J., 28
Billson, J. M., 10
Bilmes, Linda, 82

Bingham, M., 37
Binning, K., 33
Black American veterans, 79–81; adult education and, 84–86; employment for, 81; and GI Bill, 81–84, 86; healthcare, access to, 80; higher education, access to, 80, 81; housing for, 81; and posttraumatic stress disorder (PTSD), 83; and traumatic brain injury (TBI), 83
Black masculinity, 9–10
Black men, 1–2, 15–16, 49, 60, 89–90; and adult education, 89–92; counter narrative, 21–22; dominant narratives about, 16–19; and education, 6–7; employment of, 18–19; "endangered," 17; exceptionalism and postracialism, 19–21; gendered racism and, 8–9, 21–23; higher education and, 7; high school education and, 7, 18; low-income, 29; male privilege, 21; and masculinity, 9–10; stereotypical characteristics attributed to, 10, 15; and White male dominance, 29
"Blackmen," concept of, 15 16
"Black people," 8
Boes, S. R., 64
Bonilla-Silva, E., 43, 45
Bosworth, R., 59, 65
Bowles, T. A., 6
Bozick, R., 72
Brandt, D., 33
"Breadwinner/homemaker" model, 9
Bridgest, S., 33
Brookfield, S. D., 11, 22
Brooks, M., 64
Brown-Haywood, F., 60, 76
Brown v. Board of Education, 6
Bullock, L., 33
Burt, I., 64
Burton, L., 29
Butler, J., 28

Callahan, A., 59, 65
Campbell, A., 52
Cantrell, B., 83
Carter, D. J., 38
Case, A., 38

Ceja, M., 38
Census Bureau of Labor Statistics, 59
Cervero, R. M., 6, 18, 22
Chapman, C., 7
Chavez-Dueñas, N. Y., 8
Chen, X., 7
Choi, H. J., 59
Choitz, V., 59, 65
Christensen, S. L., 27–29
Chronicle of Higher Education, 5
Classroom: climate, 74–76; physical layout of, 39–40; safe, 53
Cleveland State University (CSU), 85
Clinton, Bill, 70
Closson, R., 38
Codrington, J., 91
Cohen, Leonard, 69, 76
Coker, A., 61
Colin, S., 19, 22
College Board Advocacy & Policy Center, 37
Collins, P. H., 10, 16, 23
Cool pose, concept of, 10
Cooper, A., 17
Corbin, J., 61
Cornileus, T. H., 15, 21, 23
Cornwall, A., 34
Corrections Corporation of America (CCA), 52
Cose, E., 7
Council for Adult and Experiential Learning (CAEL), 85
Counseling, participation in, 54–55
Counter-space: definition of, 38; GED® program as, 39–45
Cox, J., 9
Coyle, A., 52
Critical race theory (CRT), 5–6, 38, 50, 60, 89
CRT. *See* Critical race theory (CRT)
Cunningham, P. M., 6, 22, 23
Curriculum, for Black males, 22
Cuyjet, M. J., 2, 60, 61

Dangerfield, C. L., 29, 31
Danish folk schools, 40
Davidson, C., 59, 65
Davis, J., 9, 28, 89
Davis, L., 72
The Declining Significance of Race, The, 20
Delgado, R., 38, 50, 89

Denzin, N. K., 61
Detention centers, 52
Dill, B. T., 29
Discrimination, in employment practices, 81
Doob, C., 45
Douglass, Frederick, 50–54, 56
Drayton, B., 3, 4, 27, 36, 89, 92
Drug abuse violations, 70
Drug policies, war on, 70–71
D'Souza, Dinesh, 20
DuBois, W. E. B., 6
Duncan, G. J., 60

Economic independence, 30–31
Educational abuse, 52
Educational achievement gap, 17–18
Educational independence, 30
Educational trauma, 52–53
Einarsson, C., 74
Emotional attachment, in mentoring relationship, 43
Endangered species metaphor, for Black men, 17–19
End of Racism, The, 20
Engberg, M. E., 7
Entman, R. M., 9
Essed, P., 8
Evans, K. M., 8

Fairchild, H. H., 91
Fathering, components of, 28–29
Feagin, J., 9
Ferguson, A. A., 9
Ferrell, Jonathan, 49
Flennaugh, T., 18, 22, 23
Fleury-Steiner, B., 84
Forste, R., 28
Foucault, M., 6, 7
Frankenberg, R., 5
Fredrickson, G., 16
Freire, P., 22
Friedrich, N., 27
Fryer, R. G., 60

Gadsden, V., 27
Gangsta rap, 17
Gast, A., 59
Gavins, R., 17
Gee, J. P., 27, 31
Gendered racism, 8–9, 23

General Education Development (GED®) program, 37–38; as counter-space, 39–45; ethnographic study of, 38–39; mentoring space, 43–45; physical place and circle, 39–40; space for silence, 42–43; space for voice, 40–42
Glenn, W. J., 8
Good provider, role of, 27–29; class factor in, 29; race factor in, 29
Granström, K., 74
Grant, C., 23, 38
Graziano, J., 82
Gregory, S., 5
Griffin, K. A., 61, 62
Griffith, D., 29
Grummon, P. T. H., 59
Guy, T. C., 2, 3, 4, 15, 22, 26, 89, 92

Haddix, M., 22
Hair, E., 43
Hall, R. E., 8
Hamilton, M., 28
Hammond, W. P., 28, 31, 91
Han, M. Y., 37
Hardy, K., 54
Hargrove, D., 23
Harper, J., 91
Harper, S. R., 9, 59, 61, 62
Harris, F., 9, 59
Harroff, P., 3, 59, 68
Hauptman, A., 59, 60
Hayes, E., 22
Healing place, 42
Heaney, T., 38
Herman, J., 50, 51, 53–55
Herr, E. L., 8
Highlander Folk School, 40
High school equivalency (HSE), as counter-space, 37–45. *See also* General Education Development (GED®) program
Hill, C. T., 64
Himes, Chester Bomar, 54
Hines, G., 9
Hiring discrimination, 81
Holzer, H., 19
hooks, b., 6, 9, 10, 38, 40
Hoops, J., 59, 65
Horton, M., 40
Howard, T., 2, 18, 22, 23, 60, 65
Hucks, D. C., 2, 61

Humez, J. M., 9
Hunter, A., 28, 33
Hunter, C., 38
Huo, Y., 33
Hypersexualization, of Black men, 10

Ifill, N., 7
Imam, N., 9
Incarceration, returning to school after, 69–70; adult educators, role of, 76; advisement and counseling in college, 73; child care and employment and, 72–73; college and financial support, 73–74; and culture shock, 72–74; GED®, obtaining of, 72; and gender of instructors, 74–75; healthy classroom climate, 74–76; and meaningful curriculum, 75–76; structure and support in classroom, 75; war on drugs and, 70–71

Jackson, R., 28, 29, 31
Jarrett, R., 29
Jekielek, S., 43
Jim Crow laws, 55, 82
Johnson-Ahorlua, R. N., 62
Johnson-Bailey, J., 2, 5, 6, 11, 14, 18, 22, 53, 56, 57, 61
Jones, C., 64
Jorgensen, S., 40
Journal of Blacks in Higher Education (JBHE), 59, 60, 64

Kabatchnick, Craig, 82
Kasworm, C., 60, 63, 75
Kazis, R., 59, 65
Keating, A., 6
KewalRamani, A., 7
Kim, E., 23
Kim, J. E., 27
Kimmel, M. S., 9
King, D. K., 8
"Knees knocking," 41
Knowles, M. S., 44
Kroll, A., 52

Ladson-Billings, G., 6, 38, 45, 60, 76
Laird, J., 7
Landrieu, Mitch, 17
Lapsley, M., 56
Lasker-Scott, T., 2, 5, 14

"Learned voicelessness," 54
Lee, J., 72
Levine, M. V., 19
Levitt, S. D., 60
Levy, Y., 59
Literacy learning, 33
Loscocco, K., 28
Loving v. Virginia, 16
Luttrell, W., 27

Magnuson, K., 60
Majors, R., 10
Management and Training Corporation, 52
Manglitz, E., 6, 22
Maslow's hierarchy of need, 81
Matthei, J. A., 9
Mattis, J. S., 28, 31, 91
Mauer, M., 52
McCarthy, Barry, 70
McCray, A., 33
McIntosh, P., 5
McLaughlin, E., 49
McLeod, A., 59, 65
Menary, R., 42
Men's Lives, 9
Mentoring relationship, 43; absence of color/race blindness, 44–45; holistic, 43–44; reciprocal nature, 44
Merriam, S., 61
Merritt, Roxanne, 83
Messner, M., 9, 21
Meyer, G., 82
Mezirow, J., 11
Miles, J., 72
Miller, B., 3, 69, 77
Miller, D., 43
Miller, J., 8
Mills, C. W., 41
Miscegenation, 16
Mondesir, J., 3, 69, 77
Moore, K., 43
Moss, P., 19
Mutua, A. D., 15
My Brother's Keeper initiative, 91

Narrative of the Life of Frederick Douglass, an American Slave, 50, 53
National Academic Advising Association (NACADA), 73

National Association for the Advancement of Colored People (NAACP), 70
National Center for Education Statistics (NCES), 7
Neal, L., 33
Neofotistos, T., 37
Neufeld, R., 52
Newbeck, P., 16
New Jersey's Warren County Community College VIPER Program, 85
Noguera, P., 9, 51
Nutter, Michael, 17

Obama, Barack, 5, 49, 71, 83, 91
O'Brien, K. M., 64
Offner, P., 19
Okonofua, B. A., 8
Omi, M., 5, 8, 16
Open classrooms, 40
Orellana-Damacela, L., 7
Organista, K. C., 8
Osborne-Morris, R., 42
Ottley, A. H., 3, 79, 88
Outlaw, F. H., 6

Pager, D., 32
Palkovitz, R., 27–29
Palmer, G. A., 3, 59, 68
Palmer, P., 43
Palmer, R. T., 9
Park, J. H., 59
Patai, D., 6
"Patriarchal masculinity," 9
Patterson, M., 37
Patton, M. Q., 30
Pedagogical approach, by adult education practitioners, 22
Perceptual racism, 19
Peterson, E., 22
Piven, F. F., 83
Polite, V., 89
Portillo, N., 7
"Post-9/11 Veterans Educational Assistance Act of 2008," 79
Preciphs, T., 19
Prine, C., 82
Prins, E., 27, 33
Prison–industrial complex, 52
Professional development programs, for adult educators, 22

Quade, A., 83
Quillian, L., 19
Quimby, J. L., 64

Race: colorism, impact of, 8; concept of, 5–6; and educational practice, 10–11; in education, significance of, 6–10, 17; gender, impact of, 8–9; national origin, impact of, 8
Rachal, J., 37
Racial violence, 49
Racisms, heterogeneous, 7–10
Ransford, H. E., 8
Ray, N., 2, 5, 14
Reagan, Ronald, 70
Reconnection, 55–57
Reentry adult college student, experiences of, 59–60; barriers to reentry, 62–63; educational trajectory for Black males, 60–61; financial barrier, 62–63; implications for further research, 64–66; managing work–life balance, 63; role models, lack of, 62; sources of support, 63–64; theoretical framework related to, 60
Rich, J., 42
Riessman, C., 30
Rodriguez, A. B., 91
Rodriguez, N., 74
Rojecki, A., 9
Rosser-Mims, D., 3, 4, 59, 68, 89, 92
Ross-Gordon, J. M., 60, 61, 74, 76
Rowan, J. M., 7
Roy, K. M., 27–29
Royster, D. A., 29
Russell, K., 8

Safe environment, creation of, 51–53
Salmon run, 15
Sanjek, R., 5
Saunders, J., 72
Scarupa, H., 43
Schott Foundation for Public Education, 7, 18, 37, 59
Schwartz, J., 3, 4, 37, 39, 40, 42, 47, 51, 54, 57, 69, 70, 74, 77, 89, 92
Schwartz, P. J., 42, 49, 51, 58
Sealey-Ruiz, Y., 22, 61
Sears, D., 20
SERV Center at Cleveland State University, 84

Sheared, V., 22, 57
Shinseki, Eric, 83
Shkodriani, G., 72
Silence, as counter-space, 42–43
Skin color preference, African Americans and, 8
Sleeter, C. E., 23
Smith, A., 8
Smith, E., 17
Socioeconomic status (SES), 80
"Sociological imagination" space, 41
Solorzano, D., 38, 50
Sorg, L., 82, 83
Southern Region Education Board (SREB), 59
Sparks, B., 22
Spiritual relationships, 43–44
Spitze, G., 28
Spradley, P., 64
Spycher, D., 72
Stake, R., 30
Stater, T., 3, 69, 77
Steele, J., 72
Stephanic, J., 38, 50, 89
Stewart, A. J., 8
Strauss, A., 61
Strayhorn, T., 60
Streelasky, J., 34
Street, B., 28
Stromquist, S., 9
Struve, L. E., 9
Suarez-Balcazar, Y., 7
Sue, D. W., 41
Sullivan, A., 91
Supplemental Nutrition Assistance Program (SNAP), 71
Supportive Education for the Returning Veteran (SERV), 85
Sustained silent reading (SSR), 42

Tate, W. F., 6
Taylor-Gibbs, J. T., 17
Taylor, R., 33
Temporary Assistance for Needy Families (TANF), 71
Terry, C., 18, 22, 23
Tesler, M., 20
Tilly, C., 19
Tisdell, E., 43
Torpey, E., 86
Trauma and Recovery, 50

Trauma, impact of, on young Black and Latino males, 49–50; establishing safe environment, 51–53; findings of study on, 50–57; implications of, for practice, 57; reconnection, 55–57; recovery, stages of, 50; remembrance and mourning, 53–55; theoretical framework for, 50
Tuck, E., 37, 38
Turner, H. M., III, 27
Tyler-Smith, K., 59
Tyner, A. R., 61

Unemployment, Black male, 18–19
U.S. Bureau of Justice Statistics (BJS), 70
U.S. Department of Education, 71, 73
U.S. Department of Housing and Urban Development, 81
U.S. Department of Labor, 18

Van Thompson, C., 3, 49, 58
vanden Heuvel, K., 70
Vera, H., 9
Veterans. *See* Black American veterans
Veterans Administration (VA), 82–84, 86. *See also* Black American veterans
Vietnam War, 82
Voice, space for, 40–42

Waldinger, R. D., 8
Walker, K., 91
Walker, R., 29
Walter Reed Army Medical Facility, 82
Warren Reporter, 85–86
Washington Post, The, 82
Watkins, D., 29
Webb-Johnson, G., 33
Welfare Reform Act of 1996, 71
Whiteness, concept of, 6
White supremacist culture, 49
Wiegman, R., 16
Willson-Toso, B., 27, 33
Wilson, William Julius, 20
Wilson, M., 8
Wilson, W. J., 19, 20
Winant, H., 5, 8, 16
Wingfield, A. H., 21
Wood, J., 59, 74
Workforce, Black males in, 19
Wortham, S., 27, 33
Wright, Richard, 54
Writing: creation of space by, 40–41; silence and, 42–43

Yosso, T., 38

Zhang, J., 37

OTHER TITLES AVAILABLE IN THE NEW DIRECTIONS FOR
ADULT AND CONTINUING EDUCATION SERIES
Susan Imel and Jovita M. Ross-Gordon, COEDITORS-IN-CHIEF

For a complete list of back issues, please visit www.wiley.com

ACE143 Meeting the Transitional Needs of Young Adult Learners
C. Amelia Davis, Joann S. Olson
There has not been a *New Directions for Adult and Continuing Education* sourcebook related to young adult learners since Darkenwald and Knox (1984) edited *Meeting Educational Needs of Young Adults*. As the editors stated then, young adults are an important segment of the adult population but have received scant attention in the adult education literature. Increasingly, youths and young adults are enrolling in adult education programs and in doing so are changing the meaning of adulthood. Given the significant demographic, technological, and cultural shifts during the past 30 years, there is an increasing need for practitioners and program planners to reconsider what constitutes "adult" and "adult education." An understanding of the changing meaning of adulthood is fundamental to developing programs and policies that will address the needs of younger learners, and we believe it is time for an updated discussion among adult educators and scholars in other disciplines. This sourcebook is designed to reignite the discussion related to meeting the educational needs of young adults along with a timely and interdisciplinary discussion that highlights the transitional needs of young adult learners.
ISBN: 978-1-1189-4419-6

ACE142 Health and Wellness Concerns for Racial, Ethnic, and Sexual Minorities
Joshua C. Collins, Tonette S. Rocco, Lawrence O. Bryant
Minority status in the United States often accompanies diminished access to education, employment, and subsequently healthcare. This volume of *New Directions for Adult and Continuing Education* explores factors that have contributed to health disparities among racial, ethnic, and sexual minorities. Focused on developing strategies for understanding these disparities and promoting wellness in minority communities, the authors highlight social forces such as racism, ethnocentrism, sexism, and homophobia, which continue to influence not only access to and quality of care but also perceptions and trust of healthcare professionals. The authors identify several common themes, including the importance of communication, intentional and unintentional discriminatory structures, and perhaps most significantly, the role of culturally relevant learning sites. Scholars, adult educators, and healthcare professionals will benefit from these insights. This sourcebook is the first to address the concern of disparities and discrimination in healthcare experienced by racial, ethnic, and sexual minorities, but hopefully will not be the last to examine these issues within adult education.
ISBN: 978-1-1189-1643-8

NEW DIRECTIONS FOR ADULT AND CONTINUING EDUCATION
ORDER FORM SUBSCRIPTION AND SINGLE ISSUES

DISCOUNTED BACK ISSUES:
Use this form to receive 20% off all back issues of *New Directions for Adult and Continuing Education*. All single issues priced at **$23.20** (normally $29.00).

TITLE	ISSUE NO.	ISBN
_____	_____	_____
_____	_____	_____

Call 1-800-835-6770 *or see mailing instructions below. When calling, mention the promotional code JBNND to receive your discount. For a complete list of issues, please visit www.josseybass.com/go/ndace*

SUBSCRIPTIONS: (1 YEAR, 4 ISSUES)

☐ New Order   ☐ Renewal

U.S.	☐ Individual: $89	☐ Institutional: $335
CANADA/MEXICO	☐ Individual: $89	☐ Institutional: $375
ALL OTHERS	☐ Individual: $113	☐ Institutional: $409

Call 1-800-835-6770 or see mailing and pricing instructions below.
Online subscriptions are available at www.onlinelibrary.wiley.com

ORDER TOTALS:

Issue / Subscription Amount: $ _____
Shipping Amount: $ _____
(for single issues only – subscription prices include shipping)
Total Amount: $ _____

SHIPPING CHARGES:
First Item $6.00
Each Add'l Item $2.00

(No sales tax for U.S. subscriptions. Canadian residents, add GST for subscription orders. Individual rate subscriptions must be paid by personal check or credit card. Individual rate subscriptions may not be resold as library copies.)

BILLING & SHIPPING INFORMATION:

☐ **PAYMENT ENCLOSED:** *(U.S. check or money order only. All payments must be in U.S. dollars.)*
☐ **CREDIT CARD:**   ☐ VISA   ☐ MC   ☐ AMEX

Card number _____ Exp. Date _____
Card Holder Name _____ Card Issue # _____
Signature _____ Day Phone _____

☐ **BILL ME:** *(U.S. institutional orders only. Purchase order required.)*

Purchase order # _____
Federal Tax ID 13559302 • GST 89102-8052

Name _____
Address _____
Phone _____ E-mail _____

Copy or detach page and send to: **John Wiley & Sons, One Montgomery Street, Suite 1000, San Francisco, CA 94104-4594**

Order Form can also be faxed to: **888-481-2665**

PROMO JBNND